Catboat Summers

Catboat Summers

JOHN E. CONWAY

SHERIDAN HOUSE

First published 2003
in the United States of America by
Sheridan House, Inc.
145 Palisade Street
Dobbs Ferry, NY 10522
www.sheridanhouse.com

Library of Congress Cataloging-in-Publication Data

Conway, John E.
    Catboat summers / John E. Conway.
       p. cm.
    ISBN 1-57409-171-9 (pbk. : alk. paper)
    1. Conway, John E. 2. Sailors—United States —
Biography. 3. Catboats. I. Title.
GV810.92.C65 A3 2003
797.1'24'092—dc22   2003016118

Printed in the United States of America

ISBN   1-57409-171-9

Edited by Alex Barnett
Text design by Keata Brewer

To my decidedly better half,
Christine,
for her guidance, support, trust and love
throughout our continuing voyage together

Contents

Introduction

In the winter of 1993 our family did something impetuously reckless by purchasing BUCKRAMMER, an almost 100-year-old, leak- and rust-plagued, repair-hungry wooden boat. We then set about restoring the old bucket into our family "yacht."

What were we thinking? You hold in your hands many of the answers to this question.

In a series of short tales, this little book chronicles ten years of adventures (and misadventures) as BUCKRAMMER worked her charms on the Conways to become an integral part of our extended family. I hope you enjoy these yarns as much as we did living them.

In 1995, thanks to the encouragement of its founder and editor, Bob Hicks, the biweekly magazine, *Messing About In Boats*, began to publish my unfolding tales of our experiences. Correspondence with numerous readers of these articles led us on a journey of discovery into the historical, practical and whimsical elements associated with wearing the mantle of "historic" boat custodian (a.k.a. "reality-challenged individual"). To Bob Hicks I extend my heartfelt thanks.

I would also like to acknowledge the ongoing support of

The Catboat Association. This slightly demented group of similarly infected gaffers continues to press the cause for half-truths, poetic justice and the catboat way in the tradition of Crosby, Marshall, Williams et al.

Finally, I'd like to thank my mother and father for implanting and nourishing my love for boats and the sea at an early age, and my wife, Chris, and children, Abby, Ned and Caroline for tolerating my sometimes overly pedantic rambles on a host of nautical subjects and sub-subjects and sub-sub-subjects.

Here's to another ten years (at least!) of wonderful madness.

John Conway
Westport Point
February, 2003

1

—ᶜᵛᵛᵛᵉ—

The Family, Me and the Catboat

"We are observers, Mr. Jones, merely passing through history.
Ah, but the Ark . . . the Ark is history."
     —Belloch to Indy, from *Raiders of the Lost Ark*

"Mr. Conway, this is Richard Earle, the Westport Harbormaster, and I'm afraid we've got a problem."

Judeo-Christian genetics force me to believe that phone calls after 10 P.M. usually mean that someone or something has died.

"Problem?" I croaked.

Earle continued. "We noticed your catboat riding pretty low at her mooring earlier today and thought we'd keep an eye on her. After some supper, I took another look and saw that she was awash nearly to the coaming. I had to act fast 'cause I knew she was going down." My heart felt like a tube of toothpaste in the grip of a small child.

"Luckily we got a pump into the old bucket—the pump that hauls 200 gallons a minute—and saved her. Took the better part of a half hour at full bore. Gawd those cats know how to hold their water."

Talcum-mouthed I groaned, "What should I do?"

Earle paused. "Well, it's your call but I'd say you should come down right away. She doesn't seem to be shipping any sea at the moment . . . but you never know."

"Thanks," I squeaked. "I'll come right away."

Right away, in this case, meant tomorrow morning. Westport, Massachusetts is a good four and a half hours drive from my winter home in Summit, New Jersey, and it had already been a long day well before the harbormaster's call. I wouldn't do the BUCKRAMMER or myself any good racing up there without sleep, no matter how unsettled that sleep might be.

My mind reeled. What had gone wrong? Just a few weeks before, BUCKRAMMER, my 1908 vintage Charles Crosby catboat, had been stripped of cargo and gear for the winter. She awaited a November 8 hauling, only five days from now. At last sight, she sat comfortably unburdened on good old town mooring No. 8, just off the public dock.

Had she sprung a plank? Been holed by some reckless dolt? Vandalized? She did have a minor centerboard trunk leak, but that only amounted to less than a gallon a day. Her pumps, two automatic jobs backed up by three diesel-sized marine batteries, should have easily handled the load. Hell, they had handled this all summer like cake. What the heck had happened?

The night could not have passed more slowly. Wide-awake by 5 A.M., I dressed, packed the car with all the tools I could think to bring and hit the road.

Would the wonderful '93 season end on the bottom of the Westport River? The 300-mile drive provided the space to ponder a lifetime of events that now had me racing north on Interstate 95 this cold November Thursday.

A Lifetime in (Little) Boats

Small boats and tales of small boats have been a part of my family as long as I can remember. When I was a child my maternal grandfather would often tuck me in at night with a story or two of his misadventures off Galway Bay with his father and the family carrack "fleet":

"And just as we finished lunch, the land began to move. God only knows how we managed to spring into the boat and haul up the anchor before the whale, that we thought was a small island, dove to the ocean floor. Me pa said 'twas our campfire what's spooked him.'"

My father grew up in Hull, Massachusetts in a house right on Stony Beach, on the southern approach to Boston Harbor and near the infamous Minot's Ledge. The Conway brothers and sisters can still recite Dad's many tales from his days as a teenage lobsterman in command of a flat-bottomed skiff powered by a cantankerous one-lunger. The legendary Captain Hatch, an ontogenetic former Hull Lifesaver who almost single-handedly rescued the captain and crew of the five-masted schooner NANCY when she grounded on Nantasket Beach in the Great February Gale of 1927, often accompanied him. The melding of Captain Conway's and Captain Hatch's real and imagined adventures produced some amazing epics.

Little wonder then that Dad thought it proper for my two brothers and me to master our own vessel by the time I, the oldest, had turned ten.

Bought from her builder, a part-time shipwright who worked out of his service station in Stoughton, Massachusetts, our 8-foot, bronze-fastened, plywood wonder delivered QUEEN MARY–sized fun for many, many summers. My love for rowing with open-horned oarlocks (the only kind that Cap' Hatch would allow!) can be traced to this little, no-name pram.

When Santa brought a Sears 3 hp outboard for the NO-

NAME, we thought we had truly died and gone to heaven. For over eight years we explored the tidal waters of West Dennis, Massachusetts, from the Bass River to the Swan Pond River, in that wonderful rig.

High school brought larger aspirations. These materialized in the form of TRITON, a battle-scarred Amesbury Skiff purchased from George Klages, the commodore of the Milton Yacht Club, for the princely sum of $35. A 1956 vintage, 25 hp Evinrude acquired for $100 from "Gadabout" Gaddis (TV's Flying Fisherman!) rounded out the package.

TRITON was put to immediate commercial use as the tender for the Conway brothers' latest brainchild, Diventurers, Ltd., a scuba-divers-for-hire operation. That amazingly resilient Amesbury helped us collect more golf balls from water hazards and clean more sailboat hulls (and wallets) than you could possibly imagine. The old education fund looked pretty decent after a fashion.

By the time college loomed, I had discovered the United States government's Surplus Sales Operation, otherwise

The Conway brothers pose with TRITON in 1964. (L/R) Bob, James and the author.

known as Uncle Sam's boat (and everything else) auction department. A chance sealed bid of $327.50, my non-education life's savings at the time, won me a 26-foot diesel-powered, fiberglass Motor Whale Boat in running condition. Hauling her from the submarine base in New London to my folks' new summer place on Onset Island in Wareham, Massachusetts took a $300 loan from my sympathetic parents. (It was a boat after all.)

From her ultimate base at the Milton Yacht Club on the Neponset River, the DIVERSION would provide a remarkable ten-year education in everything from seamanship to diesel engine maintenance and repair. Our childhood pram NO-NAME and the TRITON both served as DIVERSION's tenders; the Conways almost never abandon their salty craft once possessed. This little navy gig was remarkably seaworthy but equally unsprayworthy. Our first log entry, a little ditty fashioned after Gilbert & Sullivan, reads:

> *Here's to the whaleboat DIVERSION,*
> *She'll handle the wildest blow,*
> *After her crew take an outing,*
> *They're covered with salt, head to toe.*

With college completed, the ultimate adventures of career, marriage and children squeezed boating more and more into life's bilges. It would be almost twelve years before time, tide and fortune would rekindle the flame.

Westport on the Run

"We don't get much call for marine batteries this time of year," the Sears sales clerk said doubtfully. "But I'll see what I can find down in the cellar."

My gut-wrenching drive from New Jersey to Westport had almost ended. Figuring that submersion had probably ruined BUCKRAMMER's marine batteries, I felt it prudent to pick up a spare for the pumps. I hadn't counted on the change of season to mess up the plan. No matter, I'd just buy an auto battery and a carrying strap if worst came to worst.

"You lucked out bud," the salesman clucked as he dropped forty pounds of power on the countertop. "Last one in the larder and she's all set to go."

The trip from Sears to the Point would take less than thirty minutes. The plan was simple. First, drive down to the Horseneck Beach Bridge. BUCKRAMMER would be clearly visible from that vantage point, either as a floating example of a Cape Cod catboat or as a mast truck sticking out of the river marking the shipwreck. Second, assuming the "old bucket" was still afloat, drive back to the dock where BUCK-RAMMER's tender was secured, climb in and ship out. Third, row over to BUCKRAMMER, secure the tender, go aboard and inspect the damage. Fourth, make up the rest as I went along.

Route 88 is a straight shot from civilization to the perpetually frozen past of historic Westport Point. Normally a drive south on this road has an almost magical transforming effect as you journey from the world of Internets and microchips to that of fishing nets and oil lamps. Maybe thoughts of Westport summers would help loosen the knot that seemed to tighten in my belly as the bridge got closer.

Westport on My Mind

We purchased a summer cottage on Westport Point in 1987. The Point is a registered historic village where time has come to a standstill somewhere in the 1920s. An honest-to-goodness general store, a one-person post office, a "doesn't get any fresher" fish market and a working fishing dock share Main Street with numerous buildings and homes dating back to the 1700s.

Our cottage, exposed to water on one side, sits in the middle of this Currier and Ives scene. Back in 1987, all that our new little old house lacked was a boat. This was remedied when my spouse's family generously offered dock space. The chosen craft turned out to be an 8-foot, wooden sailing pram named SPLINTER.

SPLINTER was built from a remarkable kit known as the FROG and sold by Merriman Boats of Lansing, Michigan. A clever jig system coupled with the latest in epoxy construction techniques allowed virtually anyone to build a lapstrake, spritsail-rigged sailing dinghy in a leisurely two or three weekends. Merriman even threw in all of the tools, including screwdriver, saw and awl!

My three kids, their eight cousins and about a dozen neighborhood children all took a turn slathering glue, paint and varnish during the construction phase. SPLINTER thus became one of the first wooden boats built on the Point since the whaling ship KATE CORY slid the ways in the 1800s. She is a perpetual part of summer for us Westport seasonal "turnups."

SPLINTER activated, or reactivated, the dreaded boating virus in a big way for the Conway clan, and especially in yours truly. Rowing abilities were developed or rediscovered. Sailing skills were learned and honed. (Nothing sharpens sailing skills more than tacking a spritsail pram against the current of the Westport River: You either learn to squeeze every fractional knot out of the wind or you end up heading out to sea on 2-knot ebb.) Sea legs, or at least marsh and river legs, were acquired. Valuable experience, caution, confidence and sea sense were accumulated and filed away for later use.

Unfortunately, SPLINTER seemed to shrink with each passing year. Before long it was difficult to believe that our family of five had ever been able to sail and picnic together in the little boat. The twitch to secure a bigger boat became almost unbearable.

One spring weekend, as my wife and I prepared the cottage for the summer ahead, our neighbor and sailor extraordinaire Dr. Martin Kelly stopped by for a gam.

"Hey John," Kelly teased, "did you see the ad for a Beetle Cat on the bulletin board at Lee's Market? You might be able to move up the boating food chain for a reasonable price."

I had not seen the ad but in less than an hour my wife and I were on our way to inspect HEP CAT, a 1963 vintage Beetle.

It was hard for me to imagine that I might actually own an authentic Beetle Cat. As a child spending summers on the Cape in West Dennis, I had always seen these wonderful, gaff-rigged beauties skimming along on what, at times, seemed like vapor-deep water. With one huge sail and a single "string" mainsheet, the little vessel exuded class and charm. Unfortunately, the cost of membership in Beetle-dom always seemed just beyond reach. Hell, my diesel whaleboat DIVERSION cost less than a Beetle Cat sail.

HEP CAT sat on the wreckage of a homemade trailer looking all the world like a July bonfire waiting for a match. Every galvanized screw had long ago turned to dust. Most of her ribs had split crosswise and, in some cases, lengthwise. A few planks were sprung out at angles that even Phil Bolger would find hard to design in. I felt what Joshua Slocum must have experienced when he first examined SPRAY pushing up daisies in her field on Poverty Point in Fairhaven.

However, HEP CAT's sail, spars and rigging, having been stored indoors, were in excellent shape. The deck canvas, often cracked or torn on Beetles, was in pristine condition. The coaming was secure, and the keel, skeg, rudder and centerboard seemed solid and true.

Her owner puffed on his pipe and hovered about us as we inspected the vessel. "She won the Labor Day race last year, you know," he boasted.

The 12-plus-foot Beetles are always raced with two people aboard, a skipper and a mate. I wondered who the poor bugger of a mate was in that last race. He or she must have had bailing muscles like Schwarzenegger.

"We'll take her," I said. The Conways never saw a $400 antique, wooden boat they didn't like.

HEP CAT's transformation totally consumed about six calendar weeks over June and July. Thanks to the availability of parts from the Beetle Cat Company in Padanaram we were able to replace most of the broken stuff in short order. Along the way I picked up a skill I had only read about: steam bending white oak.

After studying countless steam box designs from sources as ancient as old bound copies of *Motorboating* and *The Rudder* to the state of the art guidance of *Messing About In Boats* and *WoodenBoat*, we settled on our own version of the thing. The steam chamber consisted of a length of schedule-80 PVC plumbing pipe. The boiler was a metal gas can. A length of automobile hot water hose mated on one end to a fitting inserted into the PVC pipe. The other end connected to the flexible spout on the gas can. My white-gas WhisperLite backpacking stove provided the source of heat. We would boil up a gas can full of water on the kitchen stove. Once it was boiling, we would rush the can outside and place it atop of the WhisperLite and connect the heater hose. The camp stove maintained the boil, and steam poured out into the pipe.

The kindly folks at the Beetle Company told me to cook the oak ribs for one hour at full steam (the old rule of thumb was one hour for each ¾ inch of thickness). At first I figured that if one hour were good, then two hours would be better. Several cracked ribs later, I began to appreciate the windowy nature of the steaming art. Too little steam and the unsoftened natural lignum "glue" keeps the stick from bending. Too much steam and the lignum evaporates while the stick gets crisped. Properly steamed, the ribs went in like butter (well, cold butter).

Along with new ribs came the task of refastening. First we had to ream out the old rusty, dusty screws. Most came out in a puff of iron oxide smoke, but some of the little devils still had their screwy bite. These came along on the business end of my needle-nosed pliers. The empty screw holes were further cleaned out with an ingenious, homemade wire brush widget made for use in an electric drill and described in the excellent book *The Boatwright's Companion* by Allen Taube. Over 1,248 slightly oversized stainless steel screws went back into the holes to keep the planks from falling off, which is a good idea in a boat.

Sikaflex caulking adhesive was used to keep things watertight yet flexible. I had read in *WoodenBoat* about the Quick and Dirty boatbuilding contest wherein the contestants need to build a functional boat from a few 2 by 4s, some plywood and all the Sikaflex they want. Based on the success stories from this contest, I figured if the screws ever let go the Sikaflex alone would probably hold the boat together.

Slowly HEP CAT morphed into DRIFTWOOD, a name derived from my daughter's expressed opinion of the boat when she first saw it. The rebuilt and freshly painted DRIFTWOOD hit the water early in August, and our love affair with catboats began.

Now, as the Horseneck Bridge approached, fate was potentially about to change this love affair in a big way!

The Adventure Continues

"One *lahge regulah* coffee and a raisin scone com'in right up." The counter lady at Perry's Bakery went in the back to fill my order.

About a mile from the Horseneck Beach bridge, with images of sunken boats on the brain, I decided to take the advice of the late Tristan Jones and stop for something hot to drink. Forever getting himself into maritime trouble, Jones discovered that a hot cup of tea in the midst of a crisis always seemed to steam up a solution. I had Americanized this technique somewhat by substituting coffee. As for the scone, well, it was impossible to visit Perry's without picking up a few flour-based calories. Anyway, who knew when I'd next get a chance to eat. "Better make that two scones," I yelled.

It was good to be back in the land of dropped *R*s, added *Ah*s and missing *G*s. The coffee, scones and Westport zephyrs quickly worked their magic and before long I was back on Route 88 "walking the last mile." "Worst case," I thought, "the old girl will provide an opportunity to develop my underwater salvage skills." Amazing what a little caffeine and sugar will do.

Nonetheless, as the bridge got closer my heart continued to bang with dread. What had caused BUCKRAMMER to take on water? Why had the redundant pumps failed her? One thing was certain: If she had "bottomed out" she'd be a lot more difficult to resurrect than our Beetle Cat had been.

A Too-Tight Resurrection

In the summer of 1991, I had timed my two-week vacation to coincide with the completion of restoration work on, and the subsequent launching of, our 1963 vintage Beetle catboat DRIFTWOOD. Half of the neighborhood and most of the extended Conway clan turned out to see "how quickly she would fill and sink."

My wife's cousin Gene Kennedy had owned a Beetle named the MUTT for years. From our experience with Gene's boat, we all knew too well the early summer ritual of "swelling the MUTT" and assumed that DRIFTWOOD would also require a good soaking. The process went something like this:

1. Muster a work party.
2. Flip the MUTT bottom side up.

3. Sand, caulk and paint the bottom and topsides. Let dry.
4. Flip the MUTT back.
5. Touch up the brightwork. Let dry.
6. Trailer to Gene's sister's boat landing.
7. Exchange "sink time" wagers.
8. Launch the MUTT.
9. Time how long it took to sink. (Beetles only sink as far as their coamings, a wonderful safety feature of this wonderful boat.)
10. Settle the wagers.
11. Wait about three days.
12. Bail out, then step the mast and rig.

The need for a soak was further corroborated by numerous trips to Beetle, Inc. for restoration parts. The shop at the headquarters of Beetle, Inc. (a remarkable operation described in Waldo Howland's book *A Life in Boats: The Concordia Years*) is surrounded outdoors by Beetle Cats soaking in little "swimming pools," as my son Ned used to call them. The pools are formed by laying a plastic tarp over a doughnut of beach sand or scrap lumber that is 1 foot high and roughly 15 feet in diameter. The "soakee" is placed in the middle of the doughnut, and a garden hose introduces the water. Any fool witnessing this sight immediately deduces The First Rule of Beetle-dom: *You have to add water to the Beetle before you add the Beetle to water.*

Pop! Launching day arrived. Champagne flowed, or rather was *poured*, over DRIFTWOOD's bow. Breaking a bottle of bubbly over the little vessel would probably have brained her right on the spot. It certainly would have killed some of those in the crowd who expected a flute or two of the effervescent elixir.

"I christen thee DRIFTWOOD. Launch away." The crowd fell silent as white cedar kissed Westport Atlantic. No leaks.

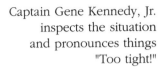

Captain Gene Kennedy, Jr.
inspects the situation
and pronounces things
"Too tight!"

"Geez Conway," Gene Kennedy taunted, "what did you do wrong?"

I wasn't sure. Five minutes had passed *and still no water.* No one had foreseen this possibility. Significant wagers hung in the balance. Ten minutes ticked by with nary a drop!

"Ya know," an old-timer piped up, "it's not nach'll that a wooden boat goes in this tight. Why I remember one of the Tripp boys losing a boat once't when her garboard plank sprung. Folks had *told* them boys that she was TOO TIGHT and, by Jupiter, theys wuz right!"

Filled with champs but deprived of a good sinking, most of the crowd drifted away after an hour or so. At least no one lost any wagers. We decided to leave DRIFTWOOD tied up to the dock for a day or two. Not that we, um, thought the planks would spring off or anything.

The Cat Sets Her Claws

On the third day following the rechristening, DRIFTWOOD still floated high and boasted a bone-dry bilge. Wondrously, the planks held tightly against her white oak ribs. My kids begged, "Dad, can we *please* step the mast and bend on her sail *now?*"

Amazed at their increasing nautical vocabulary, I relented. "OK, but everyone has to wear life jackets, at least until we know for certain that she isn't *too tight.*"

I had crewed on the Kennedy's MUTT several times over the years and felt fairly confident as to my abilities. All of which brings me to The Second Rule of Beetle-dom: *Easy to sail swell, hard to sail well.* Such was the case with DRIFT-WOOD. The first few excursions tested the mettle of both captain and crew.

The captain learned much about throat and peak halyards, topping lifts, or lack thereof, scandalizing, explosive gibes, centerboard adjustment and pinched sails. (Pinched sails? A digression: When reaching in a jib-headed boat, speed and heel angle are usually proportional to main and jib tightness, up to a point. In layman's terms, the tighter you pull in the sails, the faster the boat goes and the more it tips over. Not so with a cat! As we almost learned the hard way, pull in the sail TOO TIGHT—a different too tight—and the cat virtually stops sailing. The gaff rig likes the edge of her boom no more than a tad over the aftmost coaming.)

The crew learned to tolerate (well, sort of) the captain barking orders, gnashing his teeth and wrenching his hair. We almost changed the name of the boat to "Gan Scairteadh Amach," which is Celtic for "No Yelling Allowed!" (Which also, by the way, is the motto of the Womanship Sailing School.)

Through it all, a funny thing happened: The whole family fell in love with the forgiving and indestructible catboat. We were hooked.

The second week of vacation was filled with day trips,

twilight cruises, and nonspecific messing about. Using DRIFT-WOOD as one of the shuttle craft, a few of us Westport Point dads sponsored an overnight trip to No Name island, one of the larger rocks sitting in the Westport River. We somehow figured the logistics of moving four adults and seventeen kids plus all of the food, tents and clap-trap back and forth to that water-locked granite pile over two days and one night. (The generous use of Gene's father's 17-foot Tripp ANGLER helped considerably.)

One of the highlights of the island stay was the mastery of the fine art of *dragging*. To drag, one secures a length of line, say 20 feet, to the stern of the sailboat. With the boat moving at maximum speed, life preserver-clad children (and sometimes adults) jump one by one from the transom. Once wet, each jumper must quickly grab the trailing drag rope or suffer the embarrassment of becoming fodder for a person-overboard drill. An expert in this sport can execute the jump-and-grab maneuver in a seamless single motion (known as The Grand Turk) and be back aboard the boat in a few minutes to repeat the process. Many have jumped but few have become masters of the Grand Turk.

An August Nineteenth to Remember

Unfortunately, all good things do come to an end. Saturday arrived and with it the finish line of my vacation—in more ways than we could have imagined.

Saturday nights mean one thing on Westport Point: family square dancing! The Westport Point Square Dancing Association sets up shop from 8 to 11 P.M. in the old Methodist Church Community Hall. As corny as it sounds, nobody would miss Saturday squaring for the world. However, this Saturday's festivities were tempered by the buzz that Hurricane Bob, recently spawned off Florida, was now setting its eye for the southern New England coast. Most of us were not

even aware that a hurricane had formed. Now the blasted
thing had Rhode Island and Massachusetts in its bombsights.

The number of squares grew smaller as the evening progressed. Word about Bob was spreading, and boatowners in
the group were leaving in ever-increasing numbers. The
forecasters predicted that Bob could arrive as early as Monday morning. A good night's sleep was the best preparation
for what promised to be a very busy Sunday as boaters either battened down or hauled out. We decided to haul.

Both Beetles, DRIFTWOOD and MUTT, shared space at
Slaight's dock with Gene's ANGLER and our sailing pram
SPLINTER. On the tide, we mustered a work party and began
the hauling process.

Slaight's wharf sits in the marsh at the bottom of a gently sloped, grassy hill. On a high tide you can float the boats
ashore and use cedar rollers (i.e., round fence posts) to
move the small craft up the hill. Tom Slaight's Jeep serves as
the hauling engine.

We decided to pull the Beetles and ANGLER up to the old
apple tree where legend has it the 1938 hurricane left its
high-water mark. All loose items, as well as SPLINTER, were
removed and stored in the boathouse. The boats themselves
were secured to the ground with nylon lines tied to stakes.
Everything seemed ready for the blow. And blow it did! The
full fury of Hurricane Bob passed right through the Westport-
Dartmouth area on its way to the Cape that August Monday.
Sustained winds of 115 mph were recorded in Westport, with
gusts to 145.

We rode out the storm in our summerhouse, about four
blocks back from Slaight's, safely removed from the ocean's
fury. When the eye passed over and a brief calm prevailed,
I jumped at the chance to run down to the dock to see how
the boats had fared.

From a distance, all looked well. The Beetles were upright and roughly positioned where we left them. Gene's AN-
GLER had not moved. On closer inspection, however, it was

clear that both DRIFTWOOD and MUTT had suffered considerable damage. Large clods of grass and dirt were impaled on the tops of their masts like osprey nests. The hold-down ropes and stakes were *gone*. Apparently, the wind had blown under the boats such that they were "capsized" on dry land. On the grassy lawn you could see where the mastheads had scooped up the earth.

We speculated that when she "rightsized," MUTT's roughly ¾-inch plywood centerboard, having fallen through her trunk on the upswing, was trapped beneath hundreds of pounds of wet Beetle. As a result the whole thing had folded and snapped off on the downswing, lead counterweight, fittings and all. DRIFTWOOD's crash landing had shattered her bow. In the process, most of her too-tight planks had sprung away from the boat at the stem end. She looked all the world like a Loony Tunes Acme Exploding Cigar, after the fact. Fortunately, the rest of the boat was intact.

Well, I needed a winter project anyway.

Horseneck Bridge Ahoy!

The traffic signals at the base of the bridge snapped me out of my reverie. The moment of truth had arrived. I felt like closing my eyes. With no cars behind me, I slowed to a crawl and proceeded across the bridge. Off the road and down the embankment to the right, the village of Westport Point emerged from the trees, as did Slaight's dock and our tender SPLINTER, still tied up as if nothing had happened to her big sister.

Further along the bridge, the harbor began to creep into view. Heart and head pounding, I strained to catch a glimpse of BUCKRAMMER. For a moment, in the space where I thought BUCKRAMMER should be, I saw neither ship nor wreck. Had she submerged *and* capsized? The coffee and scones nearly came back the hard way.

Suddenly, BUCKRAMMER's masthead hove into view. Remarkably it was still attached to the rest of her mast and to an old catboat still very much afloat . . . in fact, afloat quite high above her normal waterline. Mother Nature had played one last trick on Cap'n Conway. I had arrived at the dead-low portion of a neap tide. As a result, BUCKRAMMER's mooring chain was a "longer leash" than normal, and she had drifted closer to the view-obscuring bridge. Hallelujah! Coffee and scones slowly returned to their rightful places.

Now to solve the mystery. What the hell had happened? As per the plan, I made a U-turn at the far side of the bridge and headed for Slaight's dock. When I got there I discovered that SPLINTER was nearly half full of rainwater. Her *absolutely waterproof* System Three epoxy seams did as good a job holding the rainwater in as they did in keeping the seawater out.

Rather than fool around with bailing, I hoisted the little pram up onto the dock, tipped her over and sent fifty gallons of sweet bilge water back home. I pulled the oars from beneath the seat and mounted them in the horns. I gingerly stepped in (no sense getting wet at the dock) and off we went.

This first trip would be tool-less. I just wanted to survey the damage and formulate a plan. Just a few weeks before, I had completely unloaded and unrigged the boat and stripped everything but the essentials, such as tools and fire extinguishers, in advance of her winter hauling. So my concern now focused on her Westerbeke engine and electrical system. The harbormaster's report that "she was awash nearly to the coaming," if accurate, meant that the engine and all of the power electronics were probably toast, and soggy toast at that. Whatever the case, I'd know in a few minutes.

Sklunch! SPLINTER had run aground! I used an oar to fend off of the mud flat.

Sklooch! I had done it again! Blast!

Slaight's dock lies in a small cove formed by the footing for the bridge on one side and the land of the point on the other. Just my luck! The neap tide had drained away nearly all of the navigable water from the place. Under the circumstances, the indignity of running aground a few times made the row out to mooring No. 8 much more irritating than usual. *Finally*, SPLINTER pulled alongside her older sibling, and I made them both fast. BUCKRAMMER was floating well above her normal waterline so I assumed that she no longer held much water. Nevertheless, I exited from SPLINTER as gingerly as I had boarded her. Stepping onto a seat-top in the wonderfully large cockpit that makes an old Cape Cod catboat what she is, I half expected that her cockpit sole might be awash.

Everything looked as I had left it. The engine hatch was still in place. The louvered doors of the doghouse were still closed and locked. The cockpit seats were in position, as were their cushions.

"If the water had reached the coaming, the cushions would have floated around," I thought. "Looks like Richie Earle figured the water level a bit higher than it actually was. This is good news!"

I unlocked the doghouse and swung open the doors. The floorboards and berthboards were in disarray below; clearly the water had reached berth-level. Through the skewed floorboards of the cabin sole, I could see that the bilges now held only a swish of seawater. This was in keeping with what I expected from the drip-leak near the centerboard. The automatic pump in the cabin's bilge looked fine, but I decided to remove its cover and take a look anyway.

The unit's internal float switch was stuck in the up or ON position. Obviously this little guy had experienced a high water level and had either been unable to keep up with the tide or had stuck ON until its battery had drained or its motor had burned out. I tapped the float and it flopped down into OFF. I pushed it back up expecting it to stick but it didn't. Hmmm, an intermittent failure.

"Time to see what's left of the motor," I said aloud.

A 1976 vintage Westerbeke 4-60 15 hp engine served as the boat's auxiliary. Ever since I had bought the boat, the engine had started on the first try and had run like the proverbial watch. I felt sick to think that it might now be nothing more than a mooring block in the making. Yet I did hold out some shred of hope. The same gaskets and seals that keep engine oil and water safely contained within the block can accomplish the reverse just as well. As long as the water level had not reached the air intake manifold, there might be only minimal damage. New diesels of this horsepower run about $6,000 or more, so I prayed the water had not risen that high.

The engine hatch on BUCKRAMMER is a two-part affair consisting of a large, partial cover flush to the cockpit sole and a raised box cover centered on an opening in the flush cover. This arrangement allows limited yet ready engine access through the box cover (for quick checks of oil and water levels, belts and the like) and full access to the engine and transmission with the removal of both covers. Expecting the worst, I removed both.

One Pickled Motor . . . to Go?

"I hear the old bucket almost went down!" I nearly leaped out of my skin at the unexpected sound of Mr. Bevis's voice just behind me.

"Whoa! Don't do that," I gasped.

Bevis, the harbormaster's assistant, had somehow motored his launch right up next to BUCKRAMMER without making a sound, at least to my crisis-focused ears.

"Sorry," he shot back as he advanced the throttles and pulled away.

Alone once again, I returned to the task at hand. The covers came off without a hitch exposing the little red Westerbeke 4-60 in all of its glory. Right off I could see that two batteries were gonzo. A great believer in redundant systems (from my long-ago NASA days), I had rigged the electrical system to accommodate three large marine batteries. A Guest electronic battery switch directed the charging current from the alternator and also provided solid-state monitoring of voltage and charge condition. Two of the batteries started the engine and provided power for BUCKRAMMER's principal electronics systems, such as the radio, depth-sounder, etc. One or both of these two electrical brutes also drove one of the automatic bilge pumps.

A third, more mobile marine battery was connected directly to the forward bilge pump in the cabin. This is the pump that I had earlier discovered stuck in the ON position. Through a series of more conventional power switches, this battery could also be used as an emergency source of starting or electronics power. For an additional margin of safety, this battery was mounted in a remote spill-proof box under a cockpit seat. It sat well away from its brothers and much higher above the normal waterline.

I had gone through all of this rigmarole to assure that even catastrophic flooding of the cockpit would not knock me off the air. So much for that idea.

The built-in charge indicator of the remote battery showed complete discharge. Obviously the stuck switch of the forward pump had drained the power to zero. Still, the main pump should have kicked in, as it operated on an entirely separate system.

I directed my attention to the main pump. More powerful than the one in the cabin, this unit featured an external float switch. Something about the switch caught my attention immediately. Lodged in the switch mechanism was the green plastic closing tab from a package of hamburger rolls (SELL BEFORE JULY 13). The tab had somehow positioned itself perfectly to jam the float mechanism, preventing the switch from ever turning on. You just can't make this stuff up: two pumps and two radically different, simultaneous failures. As the old saying goes, If anything can go wrong on a boat, it will. (Corollary saying: For want of a hamburger bun, the ship was lost!)

I turned to examine the remaining power elements in detail. The flooded boxes of the main batteries clearly showed that they had taken a bath. Further, in what must have been a violent reaction, the lead terminal posts and associated starting and power cables had been electrolytically dissolved, reduced to white and greenish wisps of their former selves. It's amazing what a little juice can do.

I followed the engine wiring along to the starter motor and alternator. One terminal on each of these devices had also been dissolved, if not vaporized. I dreaded to think what replacements would cost. So much for the electrical stuff.

Next on the punch list was the engine. The big question remained, Had water reached the intake? I began by looking at her oil. The 4-60 has separate dipsticks for the engine and reverse gear. I pulled the engine's stick and was delighted to find only oil. The transmission was not as lucky. I could clearly see water beads where MAX OIL should have been on the stick. Drats! OK, the transmission would need work.

Even with no water in the crankcase, I still wondered if the engine had seized. If seawater had gotten into the cylinders, the rings would probably have stopped it. This would have prevented contamination of the crankcase but still could have "welded" the pistons to the cylinder walls quite readily.

To find out, I made sure that the gear lever read "neutral," pulled off the valve cover (exposing the rocker arms and push rods) and took advantage of a neat feature of the old engine. On the front end it has a pulley wheel mounted directly to the drive shaft. I grabbed the wheel and slowly applied turning pressure. The darn thing moved! In fact, with some perseverance I was able to rotate the engine through a full revolution while observing the action of the valves. Old Red hadn't seized, at least not yet.

Right! Time to take stock. First the good news. BUCKRAM-MER was not in any immediate danger of sinking. Whatever had caused her to flood was no longer at work. (I'd come back to this mystery later.) The engine might not be a total loss. With a few new parts and some wire and oil, a test could be conducted. Finally, I now knew why the pumps had not done their job. Chalk one up to Murphy.

On the down side, the electrical system was clearly shot. It would have to be removed and replaced, batteries, switches and all. The transmission was possibly ruined as well. At a minimum, its oil (and water) would have to be pumped out and replaced, a messy job at best. Finally, and sooner rather than later, I'd have to determine where the water came from in the first place. If this happened once, it most certainly could happen again. The pleasures of boating are indeed many and varied.

The row back to Slaight's dock had an entirely different complexion than the race out. My head spun with visions of the blown weekend to come—phone calls to insurance companies, hunts for spare parts and the inevitable broadside on my bank account. I had definitely become a member of boating's Major Leagues. How had such a dumb thing happened?

Of Beetle Cats and Ice Cream Days

Hurricane Bob shut down the late summer of 1991—BOOM, just like that. With power and water out of service at the summerhouse and my continuous vacation at an end, the Conways decided to haul themselves and the wreckage of our Beetle DRIFTWOOD back home to New Jersey for the season.

Over the cold months our spirits recharged, and by Memorial Day DRIFTWOOD and the family were both ready for a ritual relaunch. DRIFTWOOD's shattered bow planks and stem had been put back aright thanks to the miracle of the Gougeon Brothers and their amazing West System epoxy products.

DRIFTWOOD and the Kennedys' MUTT were both launched on the same tide and both promptly sank.

"Hey Conway," Gene once again taunted, "now that's more like it. No way those planks will fall off from being TOO TIGHT this year." Even the legendary Sikaflex had been no match for the caulk-loosening wrath of Hurricane Bob.

The summer of 1992 was another great one for us West-point turn-ups. With two Beetles in the family, all sorts of adventures played themselves out. One that sticks in memory was the ice cream adventure to Adamsville.

The salty part of the Town of Westport, Massachusetts is formed by the confluence (I love that word) of the East and West Branches of the Westport River. On an incoming tide the West Branch current meanders along upstream toward its headwater in the village of Adamsville, Rhode Island and forms the southeastern boundary of the two states. Adamsville harbors a number of "still go'in" enterprises established at the turn of the century—the eighteenth century. These include a post office, a working grist mill (Grey's), a potter (Stonebridge Dishes), several restaurants (Manchester's and The Barn) and two general stores (a different Grey's and Simmons). Beyond foodstuffs and hardware, Simmons offers a full-service ice cream parlor as well.

Now, under the right conditions, if one is in a cruising frame of mind, and if your departure is timed just so, a Beetle Cat can enjoy both a leisurely downhill (i.e., wind abeam and tide aback) cruise on the West Branch from the Point to Adamsville, and a leisurely "downhill" jaunt back, on the change of tide. Naturally, one has to consume large doses of ice cream at Simmons to endure the drudgery of waiting for the tide to turn in the interim.

One summer Friday, just such a set of conditions presented themselves to the DRIFTWOOD, her skipper (more correctly, the man with the ice cream money), my then ten-year-old son and four of his closest buds. After a few lazy but adventure-filled hours poking our way along the river, we finally reached the landing. (One such "adventure" occurred when one of the boys discovered a bottle of nitroglycerine in the ruins of an old hunter's cabin on one of the West Branch's numerous islands, but that's another story.)

Simmons ice cream never tasted as good. Sadly, we had miscalculated the turning of the tides a tad and had to make several return trips to Simmons that day for more ice cream or potato chips or soda, while awaiting the "downhill change." Such are the vagaries of yachting, and the appetites of ten-year-olds.

We returned home close to sunset with a gaggle of sleepyheaded, overstuffed, slightly sun-roasted, catboat converts.

Now That's What I Call a Catboat!

The following day dawned as a "10" on the beach scale, so it was off to Horseneck State Park with the family for a day of bodysurfing and sandcastle building. Around 4 P.M. we reluctantly began the process of gathering up the gear and the gang when . . . fate worked her evil charm.

From out of nowhere a huge catboat, maybe a 25- or 30-footer, her massive gaff sail set for a lazy broad reach, ghosted by just outside the surf line. With the afterglow of the previous day's Beetle adventure still warming our spirits, the sight of the big cat passing seemed almost, well, mystical. My oldest daughter, Abby, and I raced down into the surf and swam out into the deep water hoping to catch a glimpse of the vessel's name and home port. Slowly her transom turned and revealed:

CIMBA

BOSTON

Magical!

We watched in wonder as the majestic thing bore off to starboard and entered Westport Harbor, about a mile or so down the beach. It looked as if she might be overnighting in our little port. The family grabbed their things and bolted for the car. We headed north on Route 88 for the Horseneck Beach Bridge hoping to see where the vessel had put in for the night from the summit of the bridge. Sure enough, there she was, tying up to a mooring just off of Tripp's Marina. It would be an easy row in SPLINTER from Slaight's dock to give CIMBA a proper Westport welcome.

A shave and a shower later, I pulled on SPLINTER's oars and headed toward Tripp's and the big cat. For this first-contact expedition I traveled solo, the rest of the family being too shy to "barge in." My camera came along for the ride to capture the moment on film. I've found the "magic box" to be a great icebreaker when meeting boating natives for the first time. What proud skipper can resist extending a boarding invitation to an admiring fan?

It worked like a charm. I soon found myself in the pleasant company of Lynda and Frank Cassidy and their daughter.

"Nice tender you've got there," Frank said as I stepped aboard.

"Thanks, I . . ." my voice trailed off. CIMBA was immaculate. Her cockpit was a tribute to the fine art of varnishing brightwork. All sails and lines were stored Bristol fashion. Everything was shipshape beyond belief. It was clear that the Cassidys were folks who took their boating seriously. With a twinkle in his eyes, Frank invited me to take a look below. Everything was in better-than-showroom order, from the classic cabin layout to the serious electronic gear, neatly organized into a miniature Mission Control.

"She's a 25-foot Fenwick Williams design, and we take good care of her," Frank explained as I exited the cabin. "But her brightwork probably needs to be reworked next spring." My mouth dropped. Museum Chippendale should look as good. The remainder of our conversation was submerged as my internal voice bellowed, "I want one of these!"

As SPLINTER took me back to Slaight's I was glad that rowing is a backward-facing sport. CIMBA, the Vision of the Surf Line, remained in sight until I rounded the Point. My family awaited the Great White Hunter's report.

You Didn't Specify English Standard

"Oooo. We don't see many 4-60s anymore." I could hear the Westerbeke parts rep at Hansen Marine scratching his head over the phone in Marblehead, some 120 miles away. "Let's see, you want a starter motor, an oil filter and an air cleaner, and you want them by tomorrow. Saturday, right? Hmm."

They say that enough money thrown at a problem usually fixes things. So, for a credit card hit larger than the purchase price of my old Navy whaleboat, FedEx and the boys at Hansen promised to have the parts in my hands by 1 P.M. the next day.

In the meantime I went to work and began by stripping out most of BUCKRAMMER's electrical system. Seawater submersion had literally turned the insides of both the starter and alternator to mush. The starter would be replaced when FedEx arrived. The alternator could wait until next year.

I installed enough new wiring to get the engine up and running safely. I appreciated the fact that, as a diesel, Old Red was more of a plumbing system than the mechanical-

electronic hybrids that gas engines have become. Using a
PAR Handy Boy pump, I next proceeded to drain the oil
from the engine and crankcase. The waste oil was directed
into a five-gallon jerry can purchased just for the occasion.

With everything more or less under control, I decided to
pay the harbormaster a visit to express my heartfelt thanks
for his actions. I also hoped that he might be able to shed
light on what conditions brought the old girl to the brink of
destruction in the first place. Westport Harbormaster Richard
Earle works out of a cozy shed at the head of the town fishing docks at Westport Point.

"My guess is it had something to do with the rain," Earle
conjectured. "We got about three inches in one shot about a
week before. I bet all of that rainwater brought your boat
down below her waterline and opened a dry seam. Once
that had happened, without pumps, there was no stopping
the inevitable."

It sounded like a plausible theory, but for one flaw.
BUCKRAMMER is equipped with self-bailing cockpit scuppers, which allow water in the cockpit to drain out
through the hull. Any rainwater should have come and
gone in one motion. Were they blocked? It was worth a
look.

FedEx came through with the parts and soon I was back
aboard. A fast check of the scuppers showed that they were
unclogged at the deck level. Yet when I gently poured a
bucket of water into each, the drains backed up within seconds, spilling their overflow into the cockpit bilge. A closer
inspection showed that the scuppers' through-hull seacocks
were closed! Like a flash it dawned on me that I had, as a
precaution, closed all of BUCKRAMMER's seacocks—engine,
galley and scuppers—when I last left her.

"Son of a gun!" Well, at least I knew where the water had
come from.

The brand-new starter slid onto its mounts like a greased
pig. Within minutes I would be able to try turning the en-

gine over. The solenoid and starter cables slipped over their terminals according to plan. The new starter had not been shipped with terminal nuts, but I thought that I could borrow those from the old motor.

Wrong! The new starter had metric threads while the original nuts were Standard. A frustrating row back to the dock and a call to Hansen Marine confirmed the diagnosis.

"We wondered about that," the Hansen rep would later comment. "The 4-60 is based on an English Austin tractor motor and sports a mix of English Standard and metric parts. No two are ever quite the same."

The two-way row, the trip to a local hardware store for metric fasteners and a stop to pick up a can of starting ether pushed the turnover test into the late afternoon. Finally Old Red was ready for a trial crank-over. I crossed my fingers and turned the ignition key.

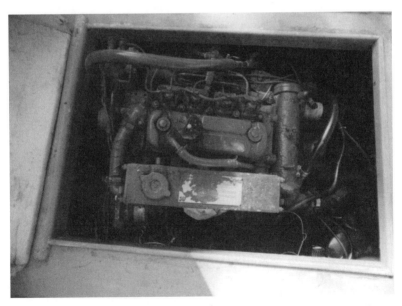

Old Red, our ancient Westerbeke diesel, awaits the verdict: Did immersion kill it?

High Tech Meets Tradition

"Geez Dad! CIMBA was featured in this issue of *WoodenBoat* last spring." Abby, my twelve-year-old daughter, waved a dog-eared copy of the magazine as she scolded me. "It might pay to open one of these copies of the mag every now and then, don't you think?"

"OK, OK, you Twinkie," I shot back. "Let me see that."

WoodenBoat is one of those magazines read so thoroughly in the Conway household that the ink usually wears off before we file the copy away as a reference. How could I have missed the CIMBA issue? I had. There as big as life was CIMBA, gracing an article entitled "High Tech Meets Tradition" (*WoodenBoat* #105). Having just filed the family-report of my guided tour of the big catboat, I read on. As my wife and soulmate, Chris, retells it, "Dad's jaw continuously dropped lower as his eyes scanned the words and pictures in that article."

Frank Cassidy, it turned out, was the Steering Committee Chairman of the 1,500-plus-member Catboat Association, and CIMBA was the group's de facto flagship. Neither Frank nor his wife Linda had mentioned these little factoids during my barging-in tour of their vessel.

"Son of a gun!" I mumbled. "Well that explains a few things."

Needless to say, the Catboat Association could not have chosen a better spokes-crew than the Cassidys nor a better spokes-boat than CIMBA. Both had hooked the Conway clan to the point where nothing else but a big old cat of our own would do.

Between the late summer of 1992 and the early winter of 1993, we took it upon ourselves to learn everything that we could about the class. Our education began with membership in the Catboat Association, a remarkable group founded in 1963 by the late John Leavens (coincidentally a fellow resident of Summit, New Jersey). The CBA has almost continuously published a professional quarterly magazine, and these numerous "Bulletins" are a wonderful source of historical and practical information. The catboat contagion expanded as our research library on the subject grew. Tomes included:

- *The Catboat Book*: An extensive compilation of the best of the CBA's historical photos and bulletin articles (available from the CBA directly).
- *Catboats*: Stan Grayson's definitive work on the subject.
- *Building the Crosby Cat*: Barry Thomas's book detailing the construction of the Mystic Seaport Museum's wonderful livery catboat, the BRECK MARSHALL (also available from the CBA).
- *The Classic Boat*: A volume in Time-Life's Library of Boating series that provides the best description of the pros, cons and techniques of sailing the classic catboat gaff-rig (out of print but commonly available through online used book web sites).
- *Nautical Quarterly* No. 11: Stan Grayson's definitive article on the subject (also out of print but available online).
- *The Boy, Me and the Cat*: Henry Plummer's delightful tale of a two-year journey (1912–13) aboard the catboat MASCOT from Slocum's Harbor, near New Bedford, Massachusetts, to Miami, Florida, and back, with one of his sons and the family cat.

On top of this research came the game of scanning the classifieds. Abby and I, in a sort of father-daughter bonding exercise, examined each new issue of *WoodenBoat* and *Messing About In Boats* as they arrived. All catboat entries were highlighted in yellow marker and prioritized as to age, builder, current location, condition and price. We wanted something big enough to hold the whole gang for at least a one- or two-night cruise and the occasional weeklong adventure. Unfortunately, our budget would only allow something in the $10,000 range. So we quickly realized that if we wanted a family-sized catboat, only "tired wood" would do.

Having already rebuilt or restored a number of boats in the "almost geranium planter" category, we were not as deterred as another family might have been. We all had developed a penchant for the smell, creak and feel of Atlantic white cedar, white oak, old pine, paint and varnish. No plastic (fiberglass) boat could come close—as long as yours truly did most of the handiwork and painting. Based on the research, we had set our caps for nothing less than an authentic Crosby catboat.

In Osterville on Cape Cod, generations of the Crosby family—Horace S., Worthington, H. Manley, Daniel, Charles, Wilton, Herbert and many others—had built catboats, mostly as commercial fishing craft, from around 1855 to around 1935. Throughout these years they had developed a reputation as premier designers and builders of elegant workhorses. Originally constructed with a lifespan of about fifteen years in mind, many Crosby boats had lasted fifty years or more. You just couldn't kill the darn things, and that was good enough for us.

Problem was, satisfied Crosby owners held onto and coddled the blessed rigs forever or until the boat finally evaporated, I guess. As a result, our Crosby quest became the proverbial search for the needle in the haystack. The January 15, 1993 issue of *Messing About In Boats* changed all of this.

Messing About In Boats Comes Through

"I think we've got a candidate catboat!" Abby was the first to spy the ad. "Looks like a vintage Crosby, Dad."

A nifty photo of a comely cat under sail graced the upper

corner of page 31, volume 10, number 17. The copy described her as 24-footer, plenty big enough for the Conway five. It claimed that she was rebuilt in 1991 (read: Hurricane Bob), but gave no indication as to her vintage. She was definitely worth a look.

Now as it turned out, the annual meeting of the Catboat Association was only a few weeks away. In my mind's eye I imagined a two-birds with one stone expedition, i.e., a weekend spent at my first catboat convention in Newport, Rhode Island, followed by an inspection of the offered Crosby in nearby Mattapoisett, Massachusetts.

The meeting was great fun, made even more wonderful by the co-ink-e-dink of bumping into Captain Cal Perkins, the owner of the Crosby in question. I wouldn't have known Cap'n Cal if I had tripped over him save for the fact that, at the meeting, he had won the coveted John Killam Murphy Award, which is given "in recognition of an individual who has advanced the principles and traditions of sail as exemplified by the Catboat Association." The ceremony was very public and visible, as was the now-identified Cap'n Cal. After the awards luncheon, I approached the skipper, introduced myself, stated my interest and pressed for the details.

"She's the CAPE GIRL, built by Charlie Crosby for one Augustus Eldridge of Chatham as the ESTHER back in 1908." Something told me that I had pulled the proverbial cork out of the bottle and was about to receive a full-draught history lesson. Cal continued without taking a breath.

"Eldridge retired the boat in 1924 and sold her to a Mr. Ferguson. We don't know much about old Furgie other than he kept the cat until 1930. That's when the William Saltonstalls of Marion, Massachusetts bought her and converted her to serve as the family pleasure yacht. They renamed her the JOSEPHINE S, after Bill Saltonstall's mother, don't you know." Cal had still not inhaled.

"The '38 hurricane washed the cat two miles inland and pretty much wrecked the whole shebang. Nevertheless,

James Coggeshall of Barnstable, Cape Cod offered to buy the remains and had his wish granted. Jimmy had the Crosby yard rebuild the girl from stem to stern. In the process she became the PELICAN. Strange name for a New England boat, eh? Yet the Coggeshalls even went as far as having a pelican figurehead carved for placement under the bowsprit. I've still got the old bird too!" Didn't this gob ever need air?

"Anyway, the Coggeshalls kept PELICAN in the family for fourteen years until 1952. From there she changed hands numerous times until I came along. I'm the eighteenth owner as far as I know. Found her in a sweet water boatyard up in Vermont. Previous owners wanted to berth her in Lake Champlain or some such nonsense but ran out of money trying to refit her. I brought her down to Mattapoisett in '85 and rechristened her with a more proper name. There she's been ever since, 'cept of course for Hurricane Bob."

"Hurricane Bob?" I queried.

Cal explained. "In advance of the hurricane I sailed CAPE GIRL down to New Bedford and secured her to a storm mooring behind the hurricane barrier there. During the blow a neighboring fishing boat broke loose, struck the old girl and rolled over her cockpit. That footloose mother-of-a-rust-bucket tore a couple of chunks out of the old girl and destroyed her steering gear to boot, but she somehow hung on. Insurance paid for a rebuild, most of which my friend Bob and I did ourselves."

I couldn't resist asking. "Quite a tale, but tell me why are you selling her?"

"I'm getting too old for this stuff," came the reply. Trouble was, Cal didn't look much older than I did.

Wincing, I asked, "When can I see her?"

Perkins beamed. "Any old time your want."

Didn't I Mention Headroom?

Soon thereafter I found myself mounting an aluminum ladder leaning against CAPE GIRL's transom. The old boat spent her winters under wraps in Cal Perkins's backyard only a block or two from Mattapoisett Harbor.

The vessel was everything I expected of a Crosby and more. She carried the fine lines of the classic cat just as described in the books: plumb stem, shallow draft (2.5 feet), full belly and barn-door rudder. Her cockpit was voluminous and could easily accommodate eight adults in comfort. All the spars were crafted of Sitka spruce and looked like telephone poles. GIRL drew auxiliary power from a 15 hp Westerbeke diesel, which started on the first try during that initial inspection. The cavernous beaded pine and oak cabin included a Dad-sized head with hanging locker, a Delft-tiled full galley, dual dropleaf tables and sleeping space for four large people, maybe even six in a pinch.

As goofy as it sounds, my heart nearly stopped when I noticed that CAPE GIRL carried an original coal/wood-burning Shipmate stove complete with copper flue pipes terminated in a classic Charlie Noble stack. Seven opening portlights, three on each side and one front-and-center, rounded out the package. My eyes glazed over.

"I'm also throwing in all ground tackle and electronics," Cal boasted. "She's a turn-the-key boat, as they say. Oh, and did I mention that she has a new sail?"

There had to be something wrong with this thing, but what?

"Would you mind if I had a marine surveyor take a look?"

Without so much as a blink Cal said, "No problem."

I had never used a boat surveyor before, but a near-disastrous experience in house buying a few years back had soundly convinced me of the value of a professional inspection. Several friends and one of my favorite wooden boat repair books, *Wooden Boat Renovation* by Jim Trefethen, had spoken highly of the legendary surveyors Captains Giffy Full and Paul Haley of G. W. Full & Associates, based in Marblehead, Massachusetts. Full, Haley and their staff, among the last of the "old school" practitioners, have developed quite a reputation in the "tired wood" department. I figured they should do the work.

Surveyors engaged, Cal chose a suitable date and the work commenced. The inspection took the better part of a day. About two weeks and about $400 later, Full's report came in. The verdict: "the vessel is at a crossroads."

In essence, the survey concluded that CAPE GIRL was in fair to good condition but showed the signs of a boat that had suffered through an extended period of benign neglect. Clearly Cal had invested a lot of time on CAPE GIRL. Yet, without fairly extensive additional care she would slowly deteriorate to the point of no return over the next ten years or so. Question was, were the Conways up to the challenge?

The family discussed the potential purchase over and over again for several weeks. Pictures that I had taken during the inspection were passed around, examined in detail and passed around some more. Discussions almost came to a halt on more than one occasion. The largest crisis revolved around my wife's innocent question, "How much headroom does she have?"

Chris had become accustomed to the sumptuous standing headroom offered by the 51-foot Beneteau we had chartered from The Moorings for family vacations in the British Virgin Islands.

"Headroom?" I squeaked. "Oh, about five and a half feet." Actually closer to 5 feet nothing. Old catboats do have this one, major shortcoming. This meant that only Caroline, at the time six years old, could stand up below decks, and at best only for another couple of years.

"John, you must be kidding!"

But somehow that crisis and several others were resolved, and the evaluation process moved toward closure.

Finally, my begging coupled with a twisted interpretation of a line taken from the movie *Raiders of the Lost Ark* pushed us over the edge:

> Belloch to Indy: *"We are observers, Mr. Jones, merely passing through history. Ah, but the Ark . . . the Ark is history."*

Call it luck or the providence of the gods or what you like, but somehow, over the years, a little wooden fishing boat named ESTHER, built to last fifteen years, had survived nearly eighty-five. Now the Conways were being offered the chance to keep this "last of breed" going, an enchanting if daunting thought. We knew this "custodianship" would require a lot of labor, love and luck, not to mention long-term financial wherewithal but, in the final analysis, it just seemed like the right thing to do. Hell, we might even learn a few things and have some fun in the process.

I made Cal an offer and CAPE GIRL was ours.

Senior and Junior Take Her Home

"Watch it, watch it," Perkins barked. "You've got to get the rear pad back about a foot more." The boat hauler from Brownell, Inc. rolled his eyes.

"Don't worry Cap, a giant egg wouldn't be in safer hands."

Moving time had finally arrived and the whole weekend promised to be a beauty, weather-wise and otherwise. The plan was straightforward. Brownell would haul CAPE GIRL from Cal's backyard over to the public landing in Mattapoisett Harbor. There we would step her mast and launch her. Once she was in the water, assuming all went well, we would rig her up and bend on the sails. Finally, after spending the night at the landing, CAPE GIRL and her crew would make their way to Westport Point on the tide.

My dad, John, Sr. (Jack) had flown in from my folks' retirement home in California for the occasion. A senior Conway just couldn't pass on an opportunity to welcome a new vessel into the clan. The launching and rigging went without a hitch even though a strong, early-May breeze made sail bending a challenge. Before long everything was shipshape and ready to go. The day had flown by, and all hands were feeling pretty good. Dad surveyed the scene.

"I've been toying with a big, bad idea," he intimated. "Any chance I could convince you to let us spend the night aboard the old bucket?" The original plan had been to sleep over at our summerhouse and then return in the morning.

"In a heartbeat!" I replied.

Smiling from stem to stern, Dad bellowed, "Then come on, we've got some provisioning to do."

Like a couple of giddy schoolkids we hopped in the car and raced back to Westport. There we picked up a couple of sleeping bags, stocked up with ice, water and breakfast supplies and grabbed a bite of supper ("You just can't get Chinese food like this in California.") After a filling meal, we zoomed back to our catboat just in time to catch sunset over Mattapoisett.

My Old Man lit the oil lamps in the old girl's cabin and made ready our bunks while I transferred our supplies into the food locker.

"Anybody home?" Cap'n Cal's ruddy face appeared in the companionway opening. "I've stumbled on a 'six-er of good luck elixir' and thought that it just wouldn't be right to drink alone." Pete's Wicked Ale never tasted better.

The evening passed all too quickly in scenes reminiscent of the shipboard overnight gam between Quint, Brady and Hooper in the movie *Jaws*. Small tales led to tall tales and then to discussions of tomorrow's homeward journey. Cal had graciously offered to accompany us ("Just so you learn a few of the GIRL's tricks), and we had gratefully accepted.

"Good night, boys. Take care now. See you on the tide."

A slightly misty-eyed Cap'n Perkins left the snug confines of the lamp-lit cabin, stepped onto the dock and headed up the gangway home.

"I don't know about you, Dad, but I'm beat," I yawned.

"That's the problem with the younger generation," my dad quipped. "No stamina. But you're the captain now, so I guess I have to turn in." Within minutes, ripsaw snoring issued from his bunk.

If the Fates had only permitted me to experience that one day and night aboard the catboat, I would have died a happy man. There in my bunk, with Dad snoring away to port, inhaling the smell of pine tar and lamp oil, rocked by the gentle motion and creak of CAPE GIRL nuzzling her mooring lines, I drifted off thinking that life just . . . couldn't . . . get (yawn) . . . any . . . better (zzzzzzzz).

"One egg or two?" I awoke to the smell of coffee perking and bacon and eggs frying over a hickory fire. Dad had fired the old Shipmate stove sometime around dawn and prepared a sumptuous lumberjack's breakfast, which he was just about ready to serve. As if on cue, Cal Perkins showed up and joined in the repast. ("Cholesterol be damned," he said, "there's something about coffee, toast, bacon and eggs that lifts up a person's soul and sends it a soar'n.")

They say that time and tide wait for no man and so it was with Buzzard's Bay that crisp, blue morning. The ebb began at 7:00 A.M. and we needed every knot it could offer if we hoped to reach Westport Harbor before twilight. It only seemed proper to designate Cal the official pilot. With an experienced hand, he took the wheel and started the diesel. The order to cast off was given and my dad and I followed through. We were away!

"With winds this light, I figure we'll motor out of the harbor," Cal suggested. "However, I have a feeling that things will freshen a bit once we're out into the bay. Then it's white sails and green water."

Cal's forecast was right on the money. As we passed the

moored schooner TABOR BOY, the flagship of Tabor Academy's fleet, and hung starboard into Buzzard's Bay, the wind picked up a good 10 knots from the northwest, an unusual but perfect wind for a full-powered beam reach—a good omen.

Orders came fast from the pilot as he headed the boat soon to be known as BUCKRAMMER up into the eye of the wind. "Hoist away, me hearties. There's wind a wasting."

We crew quickly unfastened and stored the sail cover and let loose the sail ties or "gaskets." My dad next uncleated and held the mainsheet while I manned the topping lift. With a few tugs on the lift, the vessel's 28-foot main boom pulled up and away from her aft-mounted oak crutch. The lift line was cleated off, the crutch was removed and the full weight of sail and boom now depended on the strength of 100 feet of ⅜-inch Dacron.

Scooting over to port, I quickly uncleated and manned the rig's throat and peak halyards. Threaded through an intricate yet time-proven series of sheaves and blocks (Cal did not tolerate "modern, sissified winch widgets" on his cat), the catboat halyards, with a little assist from Conway muscle, pulled several hundred pounds of sail cloth and spruce over 25 feet aloft.

"Halyards cleated off, Cal," I yelled. "Dad, you can slacken up the topping lift." I had practiced this drill in my head for many weeks.

Cal threw the wheel over hard to port and the old girl's 500-square-foot wing smartly filled to capacity. The telephone pole of a boom swung out to the appropriate length of its mainsheet, the boat heeled over ever so slightly and we took off like a shot. I was simultaneously awestruck, pleased and titillated. The spectacle of all that working wood and cloth overhead was unlike anything I had ever seen on the water.

Dad was amazed by how little the cat heeled given such powerful forward thrust. "My God!" he said, "it really is like sailing in your living room."

I looked back and saw that Cal had been studying the

both of us. He simply smiled. "Kind of humbling and grati-
fying all at the same time, isn't it?" The GIRL's former skipper
paused. "Well Mr. Conway, er, *Captain Conway*, she's all
yours." With one hand on the wheel, he stepped away from
the helm and motioned me to take over. I slid into the helm
seat and took command. Maybe life did get better!

All Good Things . . .

"You *do* know how to run breakers on an inlet bar, right?"
Cal Perkins was wearing one of his more serious faces.

"Not to worry, Cal," I flipped back. "I'm pretty sure that
with the northwest breeze blowing about 15 knots and no
ocean swell to speak of, the approach to Westport should
make a millpond seem rough."

Our wonderful Buzzard's Bay inaugural journey from
Mattapoisett to Westport was rapidly heading toward closure. BUCKRAMMER had just rounded Gooseberry Island, a
landmark that my dad and I knew as the last significant hurdle prior to making port. Mr. Perkins was not as certain as
the senior and junior Conways. "Pretty sure, eh?"

Like countless mariners before him, Cal had been de-
ceived by Westport's somewhat undeserved reputation as a
"difficult approach." Truth be told, under the right conditions
(i.e., large ocean swells, say from a storm passing south of
New England, combined with strong southwest winds on an
ebb tide), Nature does turn the peaceful seas around Westport into the hellish mess popularized by pitchpole illustra-
tions in *Chapman Piloting* and by Coast Guard photos of a
wave-engulfed Motor Surf Crasher standing upright on her
hind quarters. Fortunately, this situation only occurs on
about five widely separated days in any given year, and
today was just not one of them.

Nevertheless, our entry into Westport would not be entirely effortless. Heavy rains combined with a full-bodied

spring tide had flooded the Westport River to the limits of her capacity. All of that water was now fighting to exit at about 4 knots through a 100-yard-wide gap (sluice?) that defined the river's mouth. BUCKRAMMER's Westerbeke was about to be given her first real test under new ownership.

On top of this, the beautiful blue of the May morning's skies had gradually given way to clouds of a darkening and threatening gray. If the weather front kept moving at its current rate, we'd be lucky to reach our mooring ahead of a real downpour. Things were about to get reasonably interesting. Cal eyed the situation.

"I'd advise that we get the old girl's sail in before we attempt to shoot the rapids." My dad and I agreed. It would be hard enough for our diesel auxiliary to push against a full-force spring ebb. The added baggage of 500 square feet of canvas luffing into a strong nor'wester would probably stop us cold. We fired the engine, rounded up into the wind, reversed the unfurling procedure and, in short order, had everything tucked in and gasketted.

Her throttle advanced to half speed, BUCKRAMMER turned into the face of the white water. To port passed Mount Nubble, a large bedrock outcropping that guards Westport's western entrance. To starboard passed Half-Mile Rock, a large, semi-submerged, glacial boulder that occasionally takes nighttime yachters by surprise—the hard way.

"Looks like we're coming into a three- or four-foot standing wave situation," Dad commented. The wicked current, sculpted by the undulating river bottom, was generating a perfect train of white-capped waves that stretched 200 yards ahead across the full width of the channel. Cal instinctively increased the engine speed to three-quarters full just as the leading edge of the "rapids" engaged BUCKRAMMER's bow. Our forward movement began to drop. Cal boosted the throttle to seven-eighths full but this had little effect. A red nun buoy, almost fully submerged by the force of the ebb flow, bobbed off our starboard side but did not pass.

"I don't like to use full speed," Cal shouted. "It puts too much stress on things . . . but I don't see any other way."

He advanced the throttle to its limit. Nothing happened. At full speed ahead BUCKRAMMER was not advancing an inch and was suffering the indignity of severe buffeting from 4-foot seas on every quarter. We were on the verge of throwing in the sponge and coming about.

Suddenly my father's face lit up. He raced into the cabin and began to crank the centerboard winch.

"Blast!" I roared. In our haste to furl the sail, we all had forgotten to pull in BUCKRAMMER's centerboard: two hundred pounds of oak, bronze and lead that, fully lowered, sunk a 7-foot "brake" into the full force of the current.

Like magic, our speed increased noticeably as each inch of board slipped up into its case. Within seconds, the Old Girl kicked into high gear and leapt through the race. The strong wind and rough water flung spray everywhere. Dead ahead, where the river widened considerably, lay calm water. Yet BUCKRAMMER had to go through a minute or so more of exhilarating baptism to get there. Finally things smoothed out and the throttle was eased. As often happens in boats, in a blink a near defeat had turned into a memorable, though somewhat wet and salty, victory.

"Ahoy, Conways." Our good friend Dr. Kelly hailed us from the helm of his 13-foot Boston Whaler RIVER RAT. He had generously offered us the use of one of his unoccupied moorings while the Town of Westport decided where to permanently assign BUCKRAMMER.

Dr. Kelly pulled alongside. "Good news! I just learned that the harbormaster has assigned you to mooring No. 8, right off the main docks and an easy row from Slaight's. So, as much as I'd like you to hove up on my mooring, you can head to your permanent, new home right now if you like."

Like it we did! No. 8 was one of a handful of town-owned berths close to all of Westport's amenities (marine supply shops, post office, general store, etc.) and to our summer cottage. We had expected something closer to Cory's Island, almost a half a mile further away.

The assignment of this choice mooring seemed to cap off our wonderful adventure, but Mother Nature had one more surprise in store for us. As we snagged the mooring pendant and pulled it through BUCKRAMMER's bow chocks to a secure position on the forward bollard, a horizon-to-horizon rainbow, created by the approaching storm, illuminated the scene. My dad, Cap'n Cal, Dr. Kelly and I all just stood there staring at the sky full of colors, a tad awestruck by the spectacle. We had bested the tide and beaten the storm. Now the Westport gods seemed to be broadcasting their acceptance of BUCKRAMMER.

Meanwhile, Back in Real Time . . .

All of these past events raced through my mind as I turned the ignition key for the first time since the near disaster of a few days ago.

"runh, Runh, RUNH!!!!"

Thank goodness! With the throttle in the OFF position, Old Red had turned over. This meant that, at a minimum, the electrical system was back on line and the engine had not seized. Now for the acid test: Would the thing fire up?

I once again checked the dipsticks to make sure that the new crankcase and transmission oil levels were OK. I inspected the fuel bowl to make doubly sure that no water or air had contaminated the mix. Everything seemed to be fine. I advanced the throttle to the start position, squirted a tiny drop of starting fluid ether into the air intake and turned the starter key.

"broom, Broom, BROOM!!!!"

The engine fired up as sweetly as the first time I had started her so many months before. The tach stabilized at 850 rpm, normal idling speed, and the oil pressure read 45

psi, the typical cold-start pressure. Coolant water surged out
of the exhaust accompanied by a trace of grayish-white
smoke—all normal.

Fishermen on the Horseneck Beach Bridge, looking
down on the scene, probably thought that another boa-
towner had gone off his nut. There in BUCKRAMMER's cockpit
they witnessed a full-grown man dancing a jig to the tune of
a twenty-year old Westerbeke 4-60. The celebration lasted
about five minutes, just long enough not to jinx things.

OK, the engine had started and seemed none the worse
for wear . . . but would it continue to function? Only a good
long run would reveal that. Then there was the matter of the
transmission. It had clearly been submerged in salt water for
a spell. Would all of the myriad spinning and meshing parts
still work perfectly? Finally there was the cold reality of this
afternoon's trip across the river to the hauling ramp. Would
all of these moving parts work long enough to get me over
to the dock? BUCKRAMMER was not out of the woods yet and
a plan had to be developed to address these unknowns, but
the danged engine had started. Yes!

Phase One of the plan depended on the main engine:
Would it keep running as normally as it had been? The best
way to determine that, of course, was to let her run for an
hour or so while monitoring the gauges. If everything kept
whirling then we could move on to Phase Two, the "transmission test," and, Lord willing, a Phase Three trial run.

I took a seat next to the binnacle within eyeshot of the
critical oil pressure, water temperature and engine speed
gauges. The oil pressure had dropped to 30 psi, normal for
a hot engine. The water temperature slowly cruised through
140°F, hopefully on its way to a steady-state 185°F. The exhaust still blub-blubbed out its smoky-water mixture.

Earlier I had made another stop at Perry's bakery for a
few scones and a thermos of coffee. This seemed like the
right time to partake of these treats. The process of breaking
out the grub and smell of the Joe triggered several more

BUCKRAMMER memories from the summer of '93 that recent events had pushed to the mental back burner. There's nothing like the blending of coffee, scones and happy memories to help pass the time.

The Old Bird Flies Again

The first memory involved the creation of the Pelican Club. We had moved BUCKRAMMER from Mattapoisett in mid-May of 1993. Soon thereafter Memorial Day weekend came upon us and with it the unofficial start of the summer season. I asked Tom Slaight if we could move BUCKRAMMER over to his dock for the weekend to fit her out and, kind soul that he is, Tom agreed.

My son Ned and I marked the channel into Slaight's inlet with saplings. On the high tide, we literally followed the guideposts in and slowly motored the big cat up to Tom's pier. Gene Kennedy was first on the scene.

"Hey, Conway! I've come to make sure that your new old bucket isn't too tight." Pipe in hand Gene eyed things over. After a stem-to-stern review, he gave nodding approval when I pointed out the minor trickle of seawater seeping in by the centerboard case. "Wouldn't be a proper catboat without some kind of centerboard leak," Gene puffed.

Having passed inspection, BUCKRAMMER was now fair game for all of the Conway, Slaight and neighborhood kids to explore, and explore they did. Within minutes, my son Ned and his buddies hatched a plan.

"Hey Dad," Ned inquired, "any chance that me and a couple of the Hazletts can sleep over on the boat tonight?"

"Sure," I replied. "But a parent will have to stay aboard as well for safety's sake."

"Great!" Ned shot back. "No prob!"

Every summer my wife's sister, Mary Ann Hazlett, her husband John and their children Emily, Jed, Ann and

Matthew would visit our cottage. Summer just was not summer in Westport without the Hazlett clan. This year they had decided to arrive early in the season. Of the gang, only Jed and Matthew enjoyed the idea of sleeping in old boats. So I figured that only Ned and the two Hazlett boys would spend the night.

Little did I realize that, like some latter-day Paul Revere, Ned was spreading the word through the community of ten- to twelve-year-olds in Westport Point that the BUCKRAMMER Hotel was now open for business. Before long a line of sleeping bag–toting tots began to form on the gangplank to Slaight's dock.

"Whoa, buckaroos and buckarettes." The size of the crowd overwhelmed old Cap'n Conway. "How many of you plan to stay aboard this evening?"

Caroline snapped back, "All of us, Dad, all ten of us, and maybe a few more. Why? Is that a problem?"

"Not if you don't mind sleeping sitting up," I replied.

To make a long story short, we somehow managed to squeeze about nine crew members aboard BUCKRAMMER that

Pelican Club inaugural members included (L/R) Ned Conway, John Slaight, Liam Harty, Caroline Conway, Jill Slaight and Brendan Harty

BUCKRAMMER's cavernous interior has accommodated over 12 "club members" at one time. Here (L/R) Liam and Brendan Harty, John Slaight and Caroline Conway select prime bunks ahead of the crowd.

foggy Memorial Day night. As for the parents? Captain Conway was volunteered by the Adult Watch and Ward Society as official guardian for the duration of the "voyage." The owners of the respective children would gladly retrieve said children on the 'morrow.

The evening was passed with the usual drill of card playing, storytelling and popcorn popping. Round about midnight someone discovered the old pelican figurehead stored in the forward hatch. As the old bird was passed around, one thing led to another and the Legend of the Pelican came to life.

Seems that anyone who rubs the chin of the pelican while spending a night aboard is guaranteed safe passage through life's adventures (or something like that). Let me tell you, by lights-out time, that figurehead was one rubbed-out piece of wood. Over a breakfast of hot blueberry pancakes and cold juice, the crew decided to form the charter of the Pelican Club. To wit: "Anyone aged twelve or under who spends a night aboard the BUCKRAMMER and rubs the chin of the pelican becomes an official member of the Pelican Club and shares in the good fortune such membership provides."

The captain was commissioned by the crew to take the official photo of the charter members and to generate an official membership certificate. (Unfortunately, by the time the official photo was taken, their parents had picked up several charter members. However, I am pleased to say that the certificate was created and has been distributed to just about all of the seventeen current members.)

One of the first official functions of the Pelican Club was a visit with the now late Mrs. Marjorie Robb, a longtime Westport Point resident and one of the last living survivors of the TITANIC. This remarkable woman, twenty-four years old at the time of the sinking in 1912, entertained a houseful of Pelican Club members and their parents for several hours while posing for photos and signing autographs. She created a memory that will remain with the crew for a lifetime.

Titanic survivor, Majorie Robb, hosts the Pelican Club. (Back row, L/R) – Emily Hazlett, Mrs Robb, Matthew Hazlett, Nick Corrigan, Jed Hazlett. (Front Row, L/R) – Ned Conway, Ann Hazlett, Abby Conway.

And Then There Was Cuttyhunk

Another sip of Perry's coffee brought to mind the memory of BUCKRAMMER's participation in the 1993 Cuttyhunk Race Weekend.

Every summer Westport's Spindle Rock Yacht Club runs a sailing school for kids from about six to sixteen years old. Every other August, SRYC sailing school graduates compete in an invitational weekend race sponsored by the Cuttyhunk Yacht Club, and 1993 was a race year.

To provide room, board and transport for the racers, SRYC Commodore Philip Lee assembles a volunteer flotilla of the largest and saltiest vessels from the area. It was thus that our old Crosby cat found herself in the company of SPARTAN, the 42-foot former support tender of the America's Cup racer INTREPID, and NAIAD, William Underwood's authentic 32-foot reproduction of a Herreshoff Buzzard's Bay 25. Together we three crossed the 12-mile gap that separates Cuttyhunk Island from the mainland without incident.

Abby, Ned and Caroline hitch a tow off of BUCKRAMMER's stern.

The stony beaches of Cuttyhunk Island provide a perfect setting for day's-end cookouts.

All the boats were loaded to their respective Plimsoll lines with kids of every stripe. On the way to Cuttyhunk, many tried their hand at dragging through the cool currents of Buzzard's Bay. In fact, over the course of the three hours it took us to reach the little island, Abby, Ned and Caroline mastered the Triple Grand Turk—a yet-to-be-repeated achievement.

The races commenced around noontime on Saturday and everyone had a grand time. However, the highlight of the trip had to be the beach cookout. Around dusk, the good folks of the Cuttyhunk Yacht Club built a roaring fire on the rocky spit that forms the western boundary of the little inner harbor. An infinite supply of hot dogs and hamburgers were distributed, roasted and inhaled by the throng. Someone discovered a guitar and before long, under the spell of a picture-book sunset, everyone joined in the fun. This is what summer and boating are all about.

The Season Comes to a Close

My 1993 reverie easily burned up an hour in happy contemplation. When I snapped out of it, Old Red was still chuffing along, her gauges displaying a normal range of vital statistics. Now seemed like a good time to test the transmission.

To keep things under control, I decided to remain securely tied to the mooring during the initial tests. First I'd see how BUCKRAMMER reversed.

Old Red's shift lever was gently tugged astern. A burst of suds shot under the keel. Everything seemed to work properly. The big boat accelerated backwards and began to place strain on the mooring line. Whew! The old girl had passed the reverse test. Now for the big one.

With the engine just ticking over, I nudged the shift lever into forward. A burst of water discharged against the barn door rudder and BUCKRAMMER moved out. Still secured to the mooring pendant, the boat quickly seized up against the line. Yes! She had passed the forward drill with flying colors. It now struck me that I had not tried to restart the old engine. I hit the kill switch, waited until all breathing stopped and hit the ignition.

"Vvvrrroomm!" She fired up immediately! Phase Two had ended successfully.

To commence Phase Three, I freed up the plow anchor on BUCKRAMMER's bow roller just in case Old Red conked out and I had to anchor-up quickly. I flicked on the VHF to channel 9 in case I needed another emergency hand from Harbormaster Earle. The engine gauges were given one last scan. Everything was in order. Instinctively I took a look around for approaching traffic. It being November, all was eerily quiet.

"Well, here goes nothing," I whispered and cast off the mooring line. Scooting back to the cockpit I kicked the shifter into forward and advanced the throttle to one-quarter full.

Quick as a cat, BUCKRAMMER pulled out into the mainstream with SPLINTER following close behind. An incoming commercial swordfishing boat gave a couple of giddy blows on her horn as we passed. Her skipper came out of the pilothouse and yelled, "Good to see the old bucket under way. She gave us a good scare but I guess everything's OK?"

"Everything was OK!" I grinned back and as BUCKRAMMER headed toward the hauling ramp, I do believe that she was smiling too.

A BUCKRAMMER by Any Other Name . . .

BUCKRAMMER has worn many names over her long lifetime, including ESTHER, JOSEPHINE S, PELICAN and CAPE GIRL. When we took custodianship of the old girl in 1993 we were tempted to restore her original name of ESTHER, but obviously this did not happen. Why then BUCKRAMMER?

As I mentioned earlier in this tale, as a child I was enchanted by countless sea stories at my grandfather's knee. To counter this male-dominated situation, I suspect, my grandmother Mary McDonough Green would occasionally break in to tell the one sea tale that she knew: the true story of how her father (my great-grandfather) and his brothers built a backyard boat. From her description, the craft must have been a variation on the classic 30-foot Boston Hooker (see *American Small Sailing Craft* by Howard Chapelle).

They built the little ship behind their tenement in a space that backed up against the New Haven Railroad yards in South Boston. (Somehow they convinced the NHRR yardmaster to allow them to move the completed vessel across the tracks for launching and mooring in the Fort Point Channel, near what is now the Gillette Company's Research Center . . . but that's another story.)

My grandmother and her brothers watched faithfully as the McDonough elders assembled the boat over the course of the spring of 1908. The McDonough children used the back-yard's high wooden-slat fence as their observation platform and were forever being warned of two things as a result.

1. Don't fall off into the train yard.
2. Don't touch the buckrammers or the cayougers.

Buckrammers? Cayougers?

It seems that the water-fronted train yard had a huge problem with rats. To counter this, my grandmother insisted, the railroad had actually developed or imported an over-sized, street-smart breed of cat called "buckrammers" and an equally effective breed of dog called "cayougers." By night these animals kept the rodent population in check. By day they dozed atop the backyard fences that bordered the train yards, always looking for a table scrap or two. (From this experience my grandmother eventually referred to all cats as buckrammers.)

As a child, I always fancied that my great-grandfather's boat must have been named BUCKRAMMER (I never believed he would have used "cayouger"). In a single word "buck-rammer" seemed to somehow capture buccaneer and ham-mer, two of my favorite childhood things. In reality the boat was probably called IRISH GIRL, or something equally imagi-native.

It only seemed natural that my 1908 catboat should be called BUCKRAMMER. Somewhere the McDonough spirits are smiling, laughing or becoming more ticked off with each ac-tion I take. Time will tell.

Meanwhile, if anyone out there can corroborate any of this story of the origin of "buckrammer," or if you have a "buckrammer" derivation of your own, please write.

2

The Last Shall
Be First

Fwannah! Fwannah! The committee boat's horn signaled the beginning of the race.

"Awesome Dad," Ned hooted. "We're a good distance away from the starting line without a prayer of ever taking the lead, let alone winning. Looks like your master plan might actually work." I just smiled. BUCKRAMMER and her crew were well on their way to glory . . . er, of a sort.

The adventure had begun about four hours earlier with the provisioning of our old but trustworthy bucket with copious quantities of juice, soda, salty snacks, hot dogs and wiener buns, which would hopefully quell any mutinous thoughts among the teenaged hands. Abby, now sixteen, and Ned, fourteen, had volunteered to accompany the old man and his older nautical woodpile from our home base in Westport to Padanaram Harbor in South Dartmouth, Massachusetts, a trip of about 12 miles to the north and east. The occasion? Nothing less than the world-famous Padanaram Rendezvous, an annual race cum blowout party sponsored by the Catboat Association.

Abby repeatedly poked me in the solar plexus. "Now listen, Dad. You've (poke) got to (poke) promise (poke) that I can be back (poke) by noon" (poke, poke, poke). Abby's new job as sailing instructor at the Spindle Rock Yacht Club demanded that she put in an afternoon hitch most Saturdays during the summer.

"No problem," I promised, all the while thinking that the vagaries of sailing would make almost any schedule uncertain at best. Nevertheless our game plan *was* simple, to wit:

1. Departing at 6:30 A.M., Abby, Ned and I would sail BUCKRAMMER to the Concordia docks in Padanaram, with an estimated arrival time of 9:00 A.M.
2. Sometime around 8:15 A.M., my wife Chris would drive our family car from Westport to the Concordia facilities. Chris's planned 8:45 A.M. arrival would give her ample time to park the car, walk to the head of the dock and act as our welcoming committee.
3. After meeting us, Chris would drive Abby back to the SRYC. (And then go to the beach.)
4. Dad and Ned would search out the Race Committee (led by Marshall Marine's own John Garfield), register for the race, obtain a vessel number and receive vital racecourse vectors, then . . .
5. BUCKRAMMER's captain and crew would cast off all lines and head off to the race.

This all seemed fairly uncomplicated

"Just say the word, Dad and I'll let her go." Ned had loosened the mooring line save for a single turn. I fired up the engine, nudged the shifter into forward and barked the order to cast off. The pendant dropped away. BUCKRAMMER slowly gained speed, turned her nose downstream and sluiced onward; only 12 miles to go. Except for a frustrating lack of wind, Part 1 went fairly smoothly, albeit s-l-o-w-l-y.

At about the midpoint of our journey, just off Barney's Joy point, we ran across a 40-foot sportfisherman and her crew of six hearty souls trolling along for . . . whatever. As we passed the fishing party with all 500 square feet or so of our gaff-rigged sail let out, one of the fishermen yelled across, in a Southern accent thick enough to cut with a knife, "Whot the HE-ell kinda rig is'n that?"

Abby honked back in her most serious voice, "Mister, you are looking at the finest, handline fishing boat ever conceived by mortal man, an honest-to-goodness, gen-u-ine, cedar-on-oak, antique Crosby Cape Cod catboat." She continued, "If you hope to catch anything larger than a silverside minnow today, I'd suggest you all doff your hats and show some respect for the old girl as we pass."

All six men immediately removed their caps and saluted as we ghosted by. Ned and I looked at one another and whispered in whimsical disbelief, "Way to go, Abby." Abby returned the salute as we moved past. About a quarter mile later the stillness was broken by the sound of cheering coming from the cockpit of the sportfisherman as two 36-inch stripers were landed. Maybe there *is* something to the idea of giving catboats a little extra respect.

Better Late to Miss the Gate

Round about 9:30 A.M. our cat glided past the protective breakwater that forms the outer limits of Padanaram Harbor proper.

"You're go'in the wrong way, Skipper!" A fiberglass Marshall Cat 22 passed us to port. Her skipper, Captain Lund, hands cupped to mouth and his eyes full of business, admonished us as his craft flew by. Sure enough, the *plastic* catboat was closely followed by thirty to forty more catboats all heading out toward the starting line. The flotilla was well on its way to the line.

Abby and Ned looked at me with their famous "What is wrong with this picture?" stare.

"Not to worry," I said. "This is all part of the master plan. Look, the race doesn't start for a half an hour or so. This gives us oodles of time to meet up with your mother, drop off Abby, get our committee number and race layout and then shove off."

"Er, right!" Abby responded.

But, within a few minutes, BUCKRAMMER pulled up to the Concordia dock.

Ned hopped out, secured the docklines and scanned the area. "I wonder where our welcoming committee is hiding?" he said. Mother Conway was nowhere to be seen. "Do you think she got tired of waiting and left?"

Abby piped up. "Not a chance, but tell you what, I'll look around for Mom while you sailor boys get the number and the course map."

After some good-natured "latecomer" ribbing by the Race Committee members, Ned and I got everything we needed to be considered "race legal" from John Garfield. Meanwhile, Abby had located Chris at the water fountain inside the Concordia shop. The men and the women said quick good-byes and BUCKRAMMER zipped off to join up with the fleet.

"Hey Dad! Unless you haven't noticed, we've lost this race before the darn thing has even started," Ned complained.

I glowed with satisfaction. "That is precisely the game, my dear Watson."

"Huh?"

"Well, if the time-honored Padanaram Rendezvous race tradition holds this year, the best-est, most wonderful-est prizes will go to the *last* cat across the line. That is what you, me and BUCKRAMMER must try our hardest to secure, *last place*."

All of which brings us back to the beginning of our tale and to a point about 250 yards from the starting line with the *fwannah-fwannah* sound blaring across the water.

"You're still go'in the wrong way!"

Dozens of cats whizzed past, having crossed the line, hell-bent for the first mark. Ned and I exchanged smug winks.

"OK, BUCKRAMMER!" the racemaster called out good-naturedly. "You've crossed the line and are on the way. God-speed."

Ned took over the helm. He had been training all summer long with 420s in one of the New Bedford Yacht Club's wonderful racing programs. Now he had a chance to apply all that he had learned to a real boat.

"To make things right, we've first got to catch up with the other old wooden boats," I instructed. Ned winced, but with his competitive skill I didn't think it would be so hard.

BUCKRAMMER is one of the last fishing catboats that Charles Crosby designed and built before producing his famous "Sea" series of racing cats—Sea Hound, Sea Mew, Sea Horse and Sea Wolf. A few years back, during the first-season trials, my family had been amazed by the speed of the beamy woodpile, which typically cruised at 5 knots or better. We have speculated that many of the design elements that made Uncle Charlie's "Sea" boats nimble winners must have been incorporated into our ninety-one-year-old hull. In fact, during the previous year, under very favorable conditions, our digital speedometer had registered 9.2 knots for a few minutes on a beam reach while surfing. So we knew that the old girl had what it takes to "pick up her skirts and fly."

Slowly, we began to gain on the gang ahead. Amazingly, by the time the second mark passed astern, BUCKRAMMER had caught up with the trailing boat, a 1930s H. Winfred Crosby cat, RACHET. We waved across to RACHET's skipper Dave Hill and his family. Dave waved back. "Looking goooood, BUCKRAMMER!"

Creeping past the old cat we scanned ahead to identify the next target. A peek through the binoculars revealed DIGGER, a classic Fenwick Williams–designed cat captained by Tom Madison. Ten minutes later, Madison's fine craft was also left in our wake. Ned was doing all right for himself.

BUCKRAMMER passed two other classic gaff-riggers, CAPE LADY and AMERICAN FLYER. Soon we found ourselves somewhere in the middle of the pack.

MOLLY ROSE (left) and GENEVIEVE battle for a first (boring) place finish.

"Geez Dad! If we're not careful BUCKRAMMER might just win this thing." Interesting thought, but I knew better. The lead positions were solidly held by two impeccable boats, the Phinney/Burt cat MOLLY ROSE (Eric Peterson, captain) and H. F. Crosby's GENEVIEVE (Bob Luckraft, captain). Captains Peterson and Luckraft were among the best racing skippers in the Catboat Association, and both were used to winning the races they entered.

"Good point, Ned," I responded. "What say we break for a spot of lunch?"

"Capital plan, old bean."

I went below and gathered up our gas grill, a package of hot dogs, some rolls and the requisite condiments as Ned eased off on the mainsheet. The grill was quickly set up in BUCKRAMMER's cockpit. Before long the smell of toasted buns and grilled meat filled the air. As we lolled along, munching our way to full tummies, several of the previously overtaken vessels glided past.

"What's the matter, BUCKRAMMER?" one of the passing skippers shouted. "Did someone step on the brakes?" Ned and I just chuckled as the second round of dogs came off the spit. This strategic racing stuff was hard work.

The Going Gets Tough

We got through lunch and resisted the temptation to take a nap. After all, we did have a race to win (lose).

Ned surveyed the field. "We are clearly in last place once more, Captain. Permission granted to close up the rear and lose this thing?"

"Permission granted."

Ned Conway and the author put on the brakes for lunch during the "Last is First" race.

Ned and I both knew that a purposeful last-place finish would take a tremendous amount of skill. This was especially true in competition with the wily bunch of rogues and rascals that populate the Padanaram Rendezvous. Many of the race's participants had clinched last-place victories in previous years. Poor old BUCKRAMMER could expect her competitors to execute a barrage of cunning maneuvers and tricks in the last legs of this event. Ned and I now steeled ourselves for the coming ordeal. BUCKRAMMER rounded the second-to-last mark, and the stage was set for a contest of epic proportions.

Picture the situation: a fleet of forty or so catboats snoring along in a smoky sou'wester, with five old wooden things bringing up the rear vying for the coveted last-place position. Poetic!

At this point in the drama, allow me to hit the pause button and explain:

The Elemental U.S. Rules of Last-Is-First Racing (LIF'R)

1. No anchoring allowed (this includes drogues and sea anchors, unlike in the International Rules).
2. The vessel must continue forward movement toward the mark or line (no luffing up).
3. The sail must be unfurled at all times.
4. The race concludes no longer than one hour after the first vessel crosses the line.

Motto: Any fool can cross the line first; it takes real skill to finish last on purpose.

Now, back to the race.

Captain Tom Madison's 28-foot DIGGER led the pack toward the finish line. Close behind lay RACHET, Captain Dave Hill at the helm. These boats were followed by Cal Perkins's

CAPE LADY and by our own BUCKRAMMER, the two vessels abeam. PINKLEWINK, skippered by Bill Serle, brought up the rear, in a potentially winning position.

"Geez Dad," Ned observed, "DIGGER looks like she's giving up and crossing the line ahead of the pack."

"Don't believe that for an instant," I shot back. "Tom Madison is one of the cagiest characters afloat. And on top of that, he chose that old Down East sea dog Max Phyfe as his crewmate. That makes for a deadly combo."

Sure enough, within seconds DIGGER's crew scandalized her gaff boom, which is to say they lowered the gaff boom slightly on a tightened topping lift to spill air and reduce sail power. Looking much like a large gull with a broken wing, the old catboat slowed to the proverbial crawl while still a 100 yards off of the line: a brilliant maneuver. In rapid succession all of the other cats followed suit, all that is except PINKLEWINK. Captain Cal, his CAPE LADY a mere 30 feet off our port side, hailed my son and me.

"Yahoo! Looks like old PINKLEWINK has a jammed peak halyard and can't lower her gaff. There's no way she can slow down in time. She's a goner."

Cal was right. With her halyard stuck, the "Winkster" could not scandalize. As we watched, the full 15 knots of Buzzard's Bay breeze continued to puff out her main, and she whizzed right through the fleet to take the leading and losing position among the five. Dave Hill taunted as PINKLEWINK zoomed past, "Hey Bill! Next time oil the peak blocks before the season begins. Ha ha!" Cap'n Bill was not a happy camper.

RACHET now began a series of port and starboard tacks and jibes—the classic but dangerous "Lazy Z" tactic made so famous by the late catboat LIF'R race-ace John M. Lovens.

Ned looked worried. "I can't believe RACHET is jibing with the building southerly at her back. Cap'n Dave could really hurt his rig or himself. But I've got to hand it to him. If that big tub survives tacking and jibing all over the line, old Dave might force us and CAPE LADY into a stationary luff-up and a DQ."

CRACK! CRASH!

In a flash, RACHET experienced an explosive jibe that popped her halyard blocks right out of their bridles. With a noise that would rattle Davy Jones himself, all of her 550 square feet of sail and rig came down with a bang. Fortunately, no one was hurt by the mishap. After making sure that everyone aboard RACHET was without injury, we scooted past.

I yelled over to Dave, "Disqualified, disqualified! DQ, DQ! A furled sail puts you out of the race, buddy."

Though two of our competitors had now dropped out, a pair remained, and they were two of the most devilishly clever cats that ever ghosted along, DIGGER and CAPE LADY.

A Flag-Waving Finish

The finish line approached as DIGGER, CAPE LADY and BUCK-RAMMER, dead abeam of one another, attempted to jockey for last position. All boats had reduced sail to mere threads to minimize forward motion. Yet even with reduced canvas, wind and current conspired to nudge the old cats onward. CAPE LADY began to pull ahead by a whisker, and Cap'n Cal was noticeably perturbed.

"CAPE LADY has about a foot more freeboard than either DIGGER or Bucky," I pointed out to Ned. "And the wind has more hull to grab hold of. This will be hard for Cal to overcome."

But no sooner had I spoken these words than CAPE LADY began to drop back. Ned was first to realize how Cap'n Cal has accomplished the impossible. "That scalawag is lowering his centerboard to the max. See he's cranking the board winch."

Sure enough, Cal had completely lowered the old LADY's

board and this added just enough water resistance to impart some serious breaking action. She dropped behind us and took up the rear. With only yards to go, Cal had the edge.

"Hey boys," Perkins yelled over. "Where's the fire?"

Over on DIGGER, Tom Madison and Max Phyfe boiled. Quickly both DIGGER and BUCKRAMMER followed suit and lowered their centerboards as well. Both slowed, but the finish was going to be close. Mere feet from the line, all three vessels began to align. Cal's smile faded.

Ned broke the quiet. "Geez dad, this could end up in a three-way tie." The amazed looks from the committee boat told the same tale; never before had such an occurrence taken place. With inches to go, Racemaster Garfield raised the checkered pennant and positioned himself to end the race.

"The flags, the flags—take in the flags!" Ned shouted at me with gale force. Addled middle-ager that I am, it took me a few seconds to grasp the boy's command. Then it hit me. BUCKRAMMER flew two flags, a Catboat Association pennant aloft on a so-called "pig stick" near the masthead, and Old Glory, strung from the end of the spruce gaff boom. On our present heading, the two flags were catching just enough breeze to impart a tad of forward motion. I sprang out of the cockpit, ran forward and quickly doused the Association pennant at the mast. I then raced to the end of the main boom, uncleated the gaff flag halyard and furled Old Glory. Ned was right. Amazingly, we slowed by about a tenth of a knot.

The other boats immediately recognized Ned's tactic. Cal pulled in CAPE LADY's banners, but to little avail. Her high, wind-friendly freeboard prevailed, and she crossed the line ahead of the pack.

DIGGER's crew raced to spill her flags and pennants but, with no time left, the crew realized that her huge, gaff-mounted ensign was permanently attached—there was no halyard. DIGGER's U.S. ensign roiled and fluttered in the building sou'westerly and gently propelled the craft, ever so slightly more than ours, toward the line.

Captain Madison and his able Number One, Phyfe (a tad red from, undoubtedly, a little too much sun) looked helplessly over at BUCKRAMMER as she dropped a skosh back.

Fwannabh, Fwannabh, Fwannabh, Fwannabhbhbhbh!

The Race Committee horn let loose, and the racemaster yelled over,

"BUCKRAMMER, you're the last boat across. You win."

Ned and I danced a little jig in the cockpit. The victorious loss was ours.

Ned Conway proudly displays the "Inverted Gaff" sweatshirt trophy for capturing last place.

Epilogue

Needless to say, the wonderful Padanaram Rendezvous traditions were indeed upheld that year. To begin the ceremony, Catboat Association member and artist extraordinaire Samantha "Sammy" Smith passed out one of her handcrafted catboat watercolors to each and every race participant. Padanaram Rendezvous racers have come to treasure these wonderful gifts and the even more wonderful Sammy who, I'm told, works tirelessly to produce the forty or so paintings for this event.

For her first-place finish, in the old wood category, GENEVIEVE captured the coveted and well-deserved half-hull trophy. A number of other trophies were awarded for the first fiberglass cat across the line, for the oldest skipper and so on.

For our hard-won, last-place finish, BUCKRAMMER's crew took home sweatshirts emblazoned with the upside-down gaff sail, the traditional emblem of Last-Is-First Racing. Ned and I would proudly wear, and display these relics for many years to come, symbols of outstanding strategic seamanship and unbridled nap avoidance.

It just didn't get any better.

3

—◆◆◆—

Encounter in
Tarpaulin Cove

"Uneventful!" This one word crossed my mind as I planned the return trip from Nantucket. "Please make this journey uneventful."

Yet, as often occurs when messing about in boats, the sea gods were about to concoct a little mystery that still causes the hairs to stand up on my neck upon remembrance.

The family and I had spent the last few weekends of Indian summer exploring the nooks and crannies offered up by the coastlines of Nantucket Sound. From Monomoy Island to the east, the south Cape to the north and Nantucket and Martha's Vineyard to the south, BUCKRAMMER had carried "the little family" on a half dozen pleasant adventures. As anyone who has gunkholed in these waters knows, early fall offers uncrowded, warm water sailing with Mr. Sun still high enough in the sky to keep daylight and weather conditions nearly perfect.

We would hitch a ride with a Cape-bound friend or two each Friday evening and rendezvous with the Old Bucket in the harbor where she had been left the previous Sunday. Not having to return to our homeport of Westport each weekend allowed us to explore an area otherwise inaccessible to a crew that, at this stage in life, could only get away one weekend at a time.

Toward the last week of October, a long-anticipated but nevertheless sudden, chilly turn in the weather called a halt to our extended summer idyll. The random journey that had taken us all over the Sound ended, on that last family Sunday, with BUCKRAMMER in Nantucket Harbor with nowhere to go but home for the winter.

The following weekend found me outward bound from Hyannis, Cape Cod aboard the Nantucket ferry KIOAH. Since Conway family members are not cold weather sailors (except Dad), I would have the somewhat dubious honor of single-handing the old bucket over the hopefully "uneventful" 50 or so miles back to Westport. In other words, if everything worked according to plan, I might be able to reach homeport in a few days.

An Ill Wind Blows . . . to Advantage

The weather forecast predicted several days of fair weather with light to moderate southwesterlies, conditions typical for the Sound at this time of year. If the forecast held, this trip would be a delight.

Dusk had begun to settle in as the ferry reached the municipal pier just around the bend of Brant Point and its famous light. In a flash, I bounded down the gangplank, and jogged over to the South Street docks where, thanks to the kindness of some long-time Nantucket friends, BUCKRAMMER had been allowed to berth for the past few weeks. As I unlocked the cabin doors and scanned around, I recall thinking how perfect Nantucket can be in the off-season. The few boats that remained fit in seamlessly with the dock's picturesque surroundings. The summer crowds long gone, all seemed the epitome of the quiet Nantucket of everyone's imagination.

After rattling around in the food locker, I fired up the stove and prepared some supper. I chowed down on a filling meal of clam chowder, oyster crackers and hot tea (with a touch of milk and honey), and then turned in as the boat gently rocked me to sleep; very nice indeed.

Saturday dawned as promised by the weathermen, crisp, clear and cold (35 degrees), with a light breeze blowing toward the mainland. A quick breakfast of coffee, juice and hot shredded wheat (pour boiling water over the shredded wheat, drain, add milk and sugar to taste) got the old ticker going, and before long BUCKRAMMER and her solo skipper were underway, more or less westward bound.

The planned itinerary would take me north by north west out of Nantucket harbor, across Tuckernuck, Shovelful, Long and Hawes shoals in Nantucket Sound on a vector for East Chop on Martha's Vineyard. From there, BUCKRAMMER would shift more westerly and enter Vineyard Sound just off of West Chop (Vineyard Haven). With luck, the outgoing tide in Vineyard Sound would give the old girl an extra 2-knot boost and this, coupled with that great, beam-reaching sou'wester, would have me within striking distance of Menemsha Pond or Tarpaulin Cove by late afternoon of the first day. From either location, I could make Westport within five or six hours on the second day.

For the first leg of the trip, the weather actually cooperated. As BUCKRAMMER rounded the harbor exit, around 6:00 A.M., that wonderful light to moderate wind, so comforting and alluring at the mooring, decided to build into a bit of a howler. In no time, as we transited the coasts of Tuckernuck and Muskeget Islands, the increasing southwesterly conspired with the outgoing tide to crank up conditions perfect for a vintage Cape Cod catboat. The digital knotmeter read a steady 5.4 knots. At this rate, we might reach Westport in a single day. Yo Rinny!

We rounded East Chop shortly before noon and entered Vineyard Sound shortly thereafter. Unfortunately, the outgoing tide and the incoming wind, unlike in Nantucket Sound, had turned Vineyard Sound into a veritable Mixmaster set on puree. Not really wishing to pound my ninety-plus-year-old woodpile through 10 miles of Vineyard Sound head on, I pondered two options: turn back to Vineyard Haven or shoot over to Tarpaulin Cove in the Elizabeth Islands. Caution mixed with a desire for some forward progress made the Cove a logical choice. So I spun the helm over to 270 degrees. This set a course that would bring a wet but unpounded BUCKRAMMER into a safe harbor by mid-afternoon. So much for trying to reach Westport in one day.

A Cove by Any Other Name

Situated on the eastern shore of Naushon Island, Tarpaulin Cove has provided mariners a harbor of refuge for centuries. Its strategic position at the northern approach to the Sound served and continues to serve as a natural staging area for ships either awaiting the change of tide or holed up against southwest gales. It is said that, prior to the construction of the Cape Cod Canal, when Vineyard Sound acted as the gateway both to the port of Boston and to the open Atlantic, as many as sixty vessels might simultaneously lay over there.

Except for the almost constant, wind-blown spray across the cockpit (very cold), the broad reach across the Sound toward the cove proved "uneventful." In fact, even with two reefs tied into BUCKRAMMER's large gaff sail and with the gaff boom scandalized to reduce sail power, the boat still averaged 5-plus knots. Good old Charlie Crosby knew a thing about designing a cat. By 2:00 P.M., BUCKRAMMER had entered into the lee of Naushon and, engine engaged, motor-sailed into the Cove to wait out the blow.

It always amazes me how fast situations can change in this nautical game. One minute BUCKRAMMER, SPLINTER and I were snoring along, spray flying and a bone in our teeth, the next, almost becalmed in a snug cove. Fascinating! Anyhow, with things under control, I pottered about and found a suitable spot to set the hook for the night about 250 yards off the "south hook," near the old lighthouse on the southern side of the cove, in about 25 feet of water with excellent holding ground.

With the exception of the southernmost island, Cutty-hunk, the Elizabeth Islands are private property and mostly undisturbed. In a few locations on the private islands, Tarpaulin Cove being one, the owners allow visiting boaters to use and explore the almost virgin, white sandy beaches. Since the Fates had cast me upon one of the prettiest spots in New England, it seemed only appropriate that I should take the opportunity to row ashore and explore a bit. I whipped up a couple of peanut butter and raspberry jam sandwiches, threw them, a few Macoun apples and a bottle of Perrier into my knapsack, hauled myself, lunch and an old beach blanket into SPLINTER and headed toward land.

SPLINTER scrunched into the sand at the water's edge. I jumped out and had her pulled up on the strand and anchored, all without getting my feet wet. Though I hadn't been ashore at Tarpaulin Cove for over ten years, a quick look around confirmed that the place had not changed one iota, as they say. I had made land a few miles above an historic spot known as the French Watering Place, a freshwater spring often used by the old-timers to replenish their water casks during a layover in the cove. I thought that it would be fun to hike south along the shore of the cove to see whether the "hole" (actually a small lake) still held water. This would also serve as a quiet place to eat lunch and take a nap. To cut to the chase, the hole was still there, lunch was great and before long I lay stretched out in the sun atop the old blanket sawing ZZZs.

It took the setting sun to rouse me out of what had become a very deep sleep. Almost two hours had passed since lunchtime and the rapidly dropping temperature served as an effective alarm clock. I gathered up my stuff, headed up the beach to SPLINTER and before long found myself back aboard BUCKRAMMER.

My old Crosby catboat is blessed with a number of antique appliances capable of heating the cabin. The most efficient, low-duty chill-chasers are two, old, gimbaled Perko oil lamps. Designed to provide light, they also throw off enough heat to keep the berth area reasonably toasty. However with the forecast predicting near-freezing temperatures for that evening, I felt it was best to fall back on heating gadget No. 2, BUCKRAMMER's Shipmate coal stove. Once this little beauty is fired up (see Herreshoff's wonderful book *The Compleat Cruiser* for detailed instructions), you could literally melt lead with the heat produced—and it also cooks dinner fairly well in the bargain.

After a filling meal of beef stew with Shipmate-baked corn bread and a few hours spent catching up on some reading, I decided to turn in around 10:00 P.M. in order to get a jump on things at sunrise. The forecast called for diminishing winds from the southwest shifting to northwest by late morning. This would virtually guarantee my arrival in Westport by mid to late afternoon. Little did I suspect that my journey to homeport would bring me into a close encounter with the Twilight Zone.

On Little Cat Feet

Due to my nap, or perhaps the stew, my early nighttime sleep suffered numerous fits and starts. I woke up at 11:00, then again at 11:30, but quickly went back to sleep each time. A little past midnight, a loud noise off to starboard jolted me upright in my bunk. It seemed like the sound that I would imagine heavy chain makes spilling on a concrete floor. I hopped out of bed, slid back the doghouse roof and looked off into the night. Nothing could be seen but . . . fog! Fog?

Somehow, over the last few hours, a "so thick you could cut it with a knife" fog had moved in. How thick? Well, from the doghouse stairs, I could not make out BUCKRAMMER's glowing masthead anchor light a mere 25 feet or so aloft. Worse, the fog completely obscured the chain-rattling noise-maker, whatever it was.

As suddenly as it had started, the sound stopped and a shrouded silence descended on the scene. For about ten minutes I strained my ears listening for any hint of an abnormal sound. Except for the ripple of water against the hull and the wind slapping the halyards, I heard nothing.

I recall thinking that perhaps a large boat had anchored off near me somewhere in the misty dark. Perhaps the sound I heard was several fathoms of anchor chain spilling through a hawse pipe. It also occurred to me that it would be prudent to hoist a radar reflector up the pennant halyard as a precaution: If Tarpaulin Cove were about to entertain additional big boats, it would be comforting to know that their electronics knew that I was here. So I dug out the reflector, secured it at the mast truck, took one last look and listen around, climbed into my bunk and eased back into my cozy, down sleeping bag.

Sleep came quickly but was yet again punctuated by starts and stops—maybe it *was* the stew! All manner of strange dreams came and went. In one I recall sitting on BUCKRAMMER's bowsprit watching people on a crowded old schooner next to me eating dinner from white china and then licking the plates clean upon finishing. In another I remember standing beside an old steam railroad engine and then choking on the sooty, black coal smoke that began to billow from the funnel. In a third I found myself on a boat as it ran aground on a sandy beach in a snowstorm, whereupon about a dozen people appeared on deck only to jump overboard and wade ashore.

Dawn arrived none too quickly, but come it finally did. I lay awake under the covers steeling myself to brave getting dressed. The Shipmate stove had burned through its load during the night, and the cabin temperature had dropped somewhere into low forties territory. After about an hour of cogitation, around 7:00 A.M., I unzipped the bag and quickly threw on my clothes, along with an extra sweater. Brrrrr! Gawd! I hate cold, damp mornings.

After washing up and shaving, I opened the cabin's louvered doors, once again slid back the doghouse roof and stepped out into the cockpit. The fog seemed to have lifted a tad but had coated every surface with great beads of moisture during the night.

"Nothing that a cup of coffee and a warm breakfast wouldn't fix," I mused. About ten minutes later, coffee and hot shredded wheat in hand, I dried off the helmsman's seat with a towel, parked my posterior and began breakfast. Then the weirdness began.

Things That Go Bump

The actual encounter began with the distinct but not altogether unpleasant smell of burning coal. At first I figured that some rogue anthracite in my Shipmate stove had somehow sparked back to life, but a quick check of the firebox showed all was dead cold. Nevertheless, the smell grew more intense by the minute.

On coming back into the cockpit, I noticed that the towel used to wipe off the seat was blackened with soot. A closer inspection revealed the grime to be coal soot, heavy coal soot. And as I examined the seat further I saw that a dusting of soot and micro-cinders lightly covered the entire deck and cabintop.

"Where the heck does this mess come from?" I muttered. No wonder I had dreamed of steam locomotives; BUCKRAMMER looked like she had moored next to a particularly smoky one.

Then things got weirder. New sounds arose, not the rattling chain sound, as during the night, but sounds more like the clinking of glasses and silverware, as if a dishwasher were being loaded. These came low at first but grew gradually louder.

The downright creepiness of these disembodied sounds floating out of the fog caused me to shudder. It was the kind of shudder that one experiences when pulling cotton out of an aspirin bottle, or when someone runs his fingernails down a blackboard; the kind of chill my family has long called a winky-tink. Many winky-tinks were about to follow.

Next the voices started. Many voices, fragmented voices, voices of men and women, barely perceptible at first, but also growing ever louder. Soon, if I stretched my ears, I could make out bits and pieces.

"Mind the child . . ."

"Mr. Smith, out with ya . . ."

"—Captain, turn the [something] . . ."

This continued for about five minutes, and then it all died away as the fog once again thickened and blanketed BUCKRAMMER. In the interval, my coffee, shredded wheat and blood had all grown cold. I pondered the experience.

The clinking and voices suggested a large yacht anchored nearby (although experts often comment on how the fog can play tricks with sound and apparent distance). The people on this unseen vessel had probably just finished breakfast and were cleaning up prior to departing. Hmmm. But the coal smell and cinders threw a curve; there are not too many coal-burning boats out there. Then again, maybe this mystery boat had the world's largest Shipmate stove. Another thing bothered me: Today's sounds emanated from the port side of my boat, not the starboard side of last night. Anyway, trust me when I say that, together, the fog, smells, noises, voices and direction change, plus the lack of a companion, conspired to unnerve me completely.

For a brief moment I toyed with the thought of yelling something akin to "who goes there?" But with my luck, my neighbors would turn out to be bloodthirsty drug runners. I decided that discretion was indeed the better part of valor and clammed up.

A breeze picked up, the fog thinned and, to the east, things began to brighten. "Thank goodness," I remember thinking, "I'll finally get a chance to see what's out there." Sure enough, within minutes, the fog had lifted enough so that, if I looked out of the corners of my eyes, I could discern a shape about 100 yards off the starboard quarter, uncomfortably close to my old bucket.

Slowly, eerily, the retreating fog revealed the faint outline of a large, two-masted schooner, which I thought I recognized as the famous SHENANDOAH out of Vineyard Haven. Through the brightening air, I could just pick out the silhouettes of people walking about on deck. So much for drug runners.

Encouraged by the sight, I cupped my hands around my mouth and shouted "Hello!" No response. I tried again at the top of my lungs. "Ship to starboard, hello!" Still no response.

Then, like a slap on the side of the head, it struck me to pull out the air horn and give my fog-bound companion a loud blast, which I did. It worked like a charm. Though the fog still largely obscured the vessel, I could make out that BUCKRAMMER's blast had alerted several people to my presence, as several came over to the boat's rail and peered in my direction. Within a few seconds, an official-looking shape came to the rail, lifted an old-fashioned megaphone to his lips and yelled in an amazingly clear voice, "Ahoy vessel to port. What ship be ye and whence and whither?"

You can imagine my surprise when, as I cupped my hands around my mouth to reply, high above my head a deep voice bellowed something like, "We be the City [something]. . . . Bus out of Austin, bound for [something]. What ship be ye?"

Pivoting to locate the source of the hail, I nearly jumped out of my skin. There, to my port, not 15 feet away, was the solid, black side of a rivet-fastened steamship towering astem, astern and above my little catboat. The thing was so large and the fog so heavy that I could not make out her bow, stern or caprail, just this 20-foot by 20-foot segment of hull perilously close to mine.

Dumbfounded, I heard the "little schooner" to starboard reply, "We be the Luna . . . [something] one day out of [somewhere] bound for [somewhere] with [something] . . . ballast."

No sooner had this dialogue taken place than, as if on cue, the wind picked up and the fog swirled in thicker than ever, obscuring everything beyond BUCKRAMMER's rubrails. All went still. Quickly, my concern for my safety overpowered my amazement at the situation. If the freighter or ferry or whatever it was beside me decided to shift a tad to starboard, BUCKRAMMER, SPLINTER and Captain Conway could be squished like bugs. I sprang to the VHF radio, turned to channel 16 and sent out a message something like: "This is the catboat BUCKRAMMER, this is the catboat BUCKRAMMER, hailing any vessel anchored in Tarpaulin Cove. Come in vessels in Tarpaulin Cove."

Despite dozens of retries, no ship responded to my call. I tried channels 9 and 10, channels often used by local harbormasters in this part of the world. Nothing! Wondering if the darn thing was even working, I hailed the Westport Harbormaster. Nothing! I asked for anyone to provide a radio check. Nothing! I switched to my handheld VHF and repeated the whole process. Nothing! So much for technology. What to do?

Trembling with fear, I decided to haul anchor and motor closer to the fog-shrouded shore relying on the compass and depth-sounder. My logic went this way. The shore lay about 250 yards to the south and west. I would follow the compass in, all the while watching the sounder. BUCKRAMMER draws only about 2 feet with her board up. When the sounder indicated about 5 feet, I would set the anchor and settle down. There was no way that either the schooner or the bigger ship could operate in the shallows.

With the engine ticking over, I weighed anchor. Slowly I reversed toward the beach, ever mindful of the unseen mass just off of my starboard side. For a brief moment, I believe that I caught another glimpse of the large vessel's side or rudder but this could well have been my somewhat stressed imagination. Anyway, within a few minutes, I had maneuvered my little boat out of harm's way and into the shallows. To settle my nerves, I managed to boil up some water for tea. With a stout cuppa in hand, I parked myself on a cockpit cushion and waited to see what new treat nature had in store.

For about two more hours, until about noon, fog and silence blanketed the scene. Then, suddenly, as is often the case, the whole shroud evaporated and I found myself under crystal blue skies completely alone in the vastness of the cove, not even a toothpick of a boat in sight. Son of a gun.

A cool but not too cold zephyr built from the north. Soon it freshened into the perfect breeze for a catboat to leverage homeward to Westport. For the second time in the day, I weighed anchor and, to make a long story short, by sunset I found myself snug on our mooring off of Westport Point, a little shaken and glad to be back to reality.

Epilogue

Over the months that followed, I tried every means I could think of to identify the vessels that holed up with me in the Cove that night. No agency or enterprise queried knew of any vessels matching my descriptions operating near or about Tarpaulin Cove the weekend of October 30/31. Frustrated in my attempts, I threw in the sponge and let the hunt fade away, until . . .

Over small talk at a friend's fiftieth birthday party in late winter, I repeated my tale of Tarpaulin Cove. One individual there, Steve Wexler, a dot-com company executive, approached me after dessert.

"I couldn't help overhearing your story, and I have an idea as to how you might solve the mystery of what ships kept you company that night."

"I'm all ears," I replied. Several other partygoers gathered around.

Steve continued, "Why don't you conduct an Internet search using the name of the cove and the word fragments you heard during the cross hailing? Maybe you'll get lucky and hit a combo that points you in the right direction."

The birthday boy, Larry Maynard, suggested we use his computer and conduct the experiment here and now. A small group assembled in Larry's home office to see what might shake. We tried numerous combos without much success. Either we struck thousands of hits on totally unrelated topics or we got no matches at all. On the verge of giving up, we entered a combination something like: "Tarpaulin Cove + city + bus + luna + fog." For this sequence, only one hit returned: "Shipwrecks of Vineyard Sound." One of the group sounded a low whistle.

Somewhat taken aback, we navigated the site, a web page for scuba divers visiting Massachusetts. Within the site we found references to two disasters of long ago: the wreck of the CITY OF COLUMBUS on Devil's Bridge just across from Tarpaulin Cove (she sank on November 23, 1882, with over 100 deaths) and the wreck of the lime coaster LUNET, lost in the cove itself (she caught fire and sank on April, 13, 1898, with twelve deaths).

Larry looked up from his computer screen.

"You don't think . . . ?"

Steve said, "Well, John did say this happened on the last day in October, right?"

"So?" Larry replied.

Removing his glasses, Steve whispered, "Halloween!"

4

———⁓———

Tall Ships and Iron Men

"You're really gonna have to hustle if you hope to make the tall ships event."

Bryon Kass, owner-operator of The Engine Room, a Foxboro, Massachusetts-based marine engine junkyard, unloaded a rebuilt Westerbeke 4-60 diesel from his war-surplus tow truck. BUCKRAMMER's original but irascible "Old Red" engine had finally given up the ghost the previous season, courtesy of a cracked head. Luckily, through some mystical, astrological alignment, a reworked 4-60 had suddenly appeared at Bryon's shop. I snatched it up immediately and christened it "Red, Jr."

In theory, replacing one old 4-60 with another would be, as the saying goes, "cake." The engine mounts, prop shaft coupling and the numerous electrical, water and fuel connections would be the same. I only had to devise a way to pull the old engine out of the boat and put the new one in. Cheapskate that I am, it never crossed my mind to hire a boatyard crew to accomplish this. Instead I built an A-frame out of 4 by 4 dimensional lumber, mounted it on a half dozen cedar rollers and hung a "cheap but effective" chain fall off the cross beam to produce a homebrewed gantry crane. Bryon took a look at the sorry Rube Goldberg gantry and just shook his head.

"As I said, Mr. Conway, you need to make tracks." Kass was, of course, *more* than correct.

BUCKRAMMER and a handful of other old catboats had been invited to participate in the tall ships parade as part of the Sail Boston 2000 event. Over 100 sailing ships from around the world were scheduled to gather in Boston Harbor. We catboats would not only represent the working small craft of Boston's past, but we would also escort the square-riggers. This meant that I had less than three weeks worth of weekends to remove the old engine, install and test a new (old) engine, prep, paint, putty and provision the boat for the almost 500-mile round trip and find a crew willing to invest a week's worth of vacation to accompany the old bucket and her frazzled captain to Beantown and back. Hmmm.

First Things First

Clearly the project had to start with the engine. The old Westerbeke technical manual refers to the 4-60 as a "mini" diesel, and at 15 hp I suppose the engine is not unfairly described thus. However, the beast is just a tad more ungainly then its "mini" title would suggest due to the fact that it began life as a land-based, roughly 600-pound English Austin tractor motor. Modified for marine use with the addition of a primitive heat exchanger, a water-jacketed exhaust manifold and other sundry bits and pieces, the 4-60 also pays homage to Rube Goldberg.

It took a few hours to disconnect the original engine's plumbing and to position the A-frame, lifting slings and chain hoist. While this took place, an endless stream of bystanders and armchair quarterbacks observed, commented and suggesticated. No surprise, when it came time to do the heavy lifting, that only my trusted "cousin" Gene Kennedy and my good friend and neighbor Larry Borges were at the ready.

The removal of the engine went smoothly. Up she came out of the bilges like a radish pulled from wet soil. The cedar fence post rollers allowed us to move the motor-bearing A-frame with ease. The only moment of concern came when the engine crossed over the rear railing of the old catboat. Would it clear? It did . . . by a scant quarter inch. Maybe this *was* going to be cake. Once clear of the boat, the engine was lowered to the ground and removed from the hoisting chains. Phase One accomplished.

Phase Two consisted of preparing the old boat's engine compartment for the newer "Old Red." It's amazing what collects under and around a bilge-mounted boat motor. Aside from the usual crusty muck we found a number of old tools, dozens of nuts, bolts, screws, washers and other hardware and numerous items from past summers such as hot-dog bun bag clips, a piece of a nautical chart, a spent flare casing and so on. All of this filled a five-gallon pail with ease. Yuck!

Once we had removed all of the "artifacts," we scrubbed the area with an oil-cutting TSP-water solution and painted the entire bilge with gray work paint. The "big finish" of Phase Two came with the installation of a copper drip pan within which the engine would sit. Old marine engines, the 4-60 especially, are notorious oil leakers. We hoped that our rebuilt machine would not be so inclined, but I felt that this was a good opportunity to install a little bit of preventive hardware just in case.

After a few hours of messy but rewarding work, BUCK-RAMMER's "engine room" looked shipshape and Bristol fashion. Phase Three, the installation of Red, Jr. would take place "on the 'morrow."

Crash and Scrunch

The next morning literally came with a bang. We had placed Red, Jr. on a set of four sawhorses just behind BUCKRAMMER's stern in preparation for the installation. There it had sat for several days without a peep. But just as dawn broke on the day of Phase Three, one of the horses decided to fall down on the job and took with it the other horses and the engine.

Crunch!

I sat bolt upright in my bed and immediately suspected the worst. (We keep BUCKRAMMER next to our summerhouse and just outside of our bedroom window.) Racing outside in my boxers, I found "Jr." burrowed three inches into the ground, on its side and surrounded by sawhorse wreckage. Diesel oil dripped from a secondary fuel filter that had both popped out of its holder and scooped up a clod of soil.

Groan!

I single-handedly repositioned the A-frame, attached lifting slings to Jr.'s lift points, clipped on the chain falls and hoisted away. This was *really* like pulling a radish out of wet soil. A quick inspection revealed that no serious harm had been done . . . at least to the naked eye. Damage seemed confined to the fuel filter assembly. This is a collection of copper lines, rubber hoses and cartridge filters that serves as the last stop for fuel before it reaches the injection pump. The engine must have landed directly on this area. Most everything there was a hopeless tangle of twisted, crimped, bent or leaking parts.

Blast!

Chris brought out a cup of coffee and asked, "Is the patient terminal?"

"I don't think so," I replied. "But I'm not sure that I can repair the damage in time for the tall ships event."

After a pause and a few sips of Joe, Chris said, "I thought that the old engine was the same as this one? If so, why not just strip the parts you need off of the original engine and put them on the new one?"

A great weight lifted. "Oh course! Chris, you are a genius!"

"OK, lover boy. Glad I could help. Now this genius is going back to bed for an hour or so. Don't wake me up."

I quietly changed into some work clothes and began the operation on Sr. and Jr. In less than an hour, the transplant had been accomplished.

"Ready for Phase Three?" Right on time, Gene and Larry came by to help install Jr. They were dumbfounded to learn of the near disaster, but were very impressed by Chris's quick thinking.

Gene commented, "You'll never live down a girl fixing the engine, old bean."

The three of us hoisted the rebuilt engine over the transom and into position above the engine bed and mounts. We then lowered the beast, only to find that the holes in the mounts were too small for the mounting studs. Gene deduced the problem.

"I bet the new engine has metric holes." A quick measurement confirmed this. The Westerbeke 4-60 is notorious for mixing metric and English Standard fittings. Apparently the mounts on Jr. were metric while the mounts on Sr. were otherwise. But with Chris's words still echoing in my mind I said, "No problem! We'll just remove the brackets from the old engine and switch them for those on the new engine. Cake!"

Amazingly, it worked. Within an hour Jr. was installed, reconnected (except for the prop shaft) and ready for a test crank. Maybe we *would* make the tall ships parade.

One Last Hurdle

In comparison to the engine project, the rest of the outfitting went remarkably well. The weather continued sunny and warm throughout the period, which allowed us to scrape, paint and pretty up the old girl. With one week to spare, BUCKRAMMER found herself sitting in the water at Slaight's dock, soaking and tightening up her seams and settling in for a great adventure.

I had also been lucky enough to arrange an "up to Boston" crew. Haydn Samuel, an excellent sailor and long-time friend would drive in from Pennsylvania. He would stay with the boat from Westport to Boston. Larry Borges had also somehow found time to journey with us from Westport to Boston. Leo Donahue, yet another old friend and sailor, would join the gang midway. Chris referred to the arrangement as "The Three Musketeers and D'Artagnan" (she never did reveal who was D'Artagnan). The professions of these individuals also worked out quite nicely: Haydn owns an insurance adjusting firm, Larry is a neurosurgeon at the Massachusetts General Hospital, Leo is a bank president and I'm an engineer. I figured that together we had all of the disciplines necessary to cover any contingency. Little did I realize that we would need the services of a politician as well.

Only one hurdle remained: I had yet to connect the prop shaft and run the new engine. Old wooden boats are really meant to be kept in the water, but this is somewhat impractical in our situation. During the winter months, while "on the hard" (land), the boat's hull dries out, and the wood twists and turns as it does so. To keep the propeller shaft from being bent, we routinely disconnect it in the fall and do not reconnect it until the boat has been relaunched and has had a chance to settle into its "wet shape." This takes about three days in BUCKRAMMER's case.

So, on the fourth day after launch, on the eve of our journey from Westport to Boston Harbor, I connected the shaft and cranked the engine. The motor turned over but did not start. More cranking! More nothing!

A diesel engine is a pretty simple gadget—basically a macroscopic plumbing system. Fuel is injected into the cylinders; the cylinders compress the fuel to the point of ignition; smoke exhausts; power is produced and the cycle continues. When a diesel engine does not run, it usually means that fuel is not reaching the cylinders. With this in mind, beginning at the fuel-tank end of the system, I began to troubleshoot. After a half hour of poking about, I had learned that fuel was making its way from the tank to the first filter, from the first filter to the primer pump, from the primer pump to the secondary filter (the part that we had replaced) and from the secondary filter to the fuel pump. However, when I pulled the injector lines off of the injectors, the lines remained dry. (They should look like four squirt guns shooting fuel as the engine cranks.) Clearly something was amiss with the fuel pump. A quick review of the engine manual revealed several potential problems:

1. The pump's fuel-stop lever was in the OFF position—easy to fix.
2. The speed control assembly was broken—very expensive to fix.
3. The fuel injection section was dead, maybe due to the fall—very expensive to fix.

Drats!

Statistically, this problem was going to cost me. Undaunted I checked to see whether the fuel stop was in the run position (it was). That left items 2 and 3. These would require the removal of the pump. Double drats!

It took about thirty minutes more to pull the pump from the engine. As I was placing the liberated pump on the deck, I heard a noise from within. A little shake of the unit confirmed that something was rattling around inside. I consulted the manual and discovered that a ballpoint pen–sized spring controlled the fuel stop from within the pump. If the spring popped off, then the fuel stop jumped to the "No Fuel" position. Could this be the problem? I removed a little cover plate on the side of the pump and the spring rolled out into my hands. It *had* come off. With the help of a set of needle nose pliers and a huge dollop of luck, I reconnected the spring, reinstalled and timed the pump, primed the system with fuel and bled the air out of the whole shebang.

Fingers and toes crossed, I engaged the starter motor. In less than a second, Jr. fired up and began to run like the proverbial watch. I danced a little jig in the cockpit. It's amazing to think that BUCKRAMMER's entire auxiliary power system depends on a spring the size of a paperclip.

Off to Boston

Finally the morning of our departure arrived clear and warm with a modest breeze from the southwest. I still couldn't believe that everything had somehow come together. The boat looked great and ran beautifully. Haydn and Larry were as excited as Cub Scouts on their first overnight camping trip. I was reasonably cool and collected on the outside but was a bundle of nerves on the inside. I kept running over multiple mental checklists covering food, navigation, weather, first aid and so on. My children call this my "Boating Mother Hen Syndrome."

A little send-off party of friends and family waved us out. If all went according to plan, BUCKRAMMER would not return for a few, glorious, historic weeks. With the help of an outgoing tide we cleared the Nubble entrance to Westport Harbor in record time and pointed our old catboat north by east.

The route to Boston Harbor would take us north through Buzzard's Bay to Onset Harbor, just west of the land portion of the Cape Cod Canal. Here we would pick up Leo Donahue. Together, BUCKRAMMER's captain and mates would shoot east through the canal into Cape Cod Bay. From there, we would head due north to Scituate Harbor, just south of Boston. The last leg of the trip would take us from Scituate, past Minot's Light, into Boston's outer harbor and then south into Hull Bay. The wonderful people of the Hull Yacht Club had volunteered to host us during the event. They had placed the full services of their facility at our disposal at no charge.

Under sail and power and with the cooperation of the weather, it is possible to make this journey in two days' time. However we decided to take a more "gentlemanly" three or four days. As long as we were in Boston in time for the parade on July 10, all would be well.

Larry, Haydn and I fell into the routine of catboaters on vacation within an hour of our departure; that is, we were "like totally chilled out, man." With the wind on our beam and fair seas, the boat would almost sail herself. So we broke out the fishing rods, binoculars and other essential recreational paraphernalia.

BUCKRAMMER sits on her mooring at Westport Point prior to her tall ships adventure.

A global positioning system (GPS) receiver had worked its way into BUCKRAMMER's kit as one of the new gadgets aboard. I had convinced Chris that, for safety purposes of course, BUCKRAMMER would need to be outfitted with a GPS system for the trip. Based on a strong recommendation from *Practical Sailor* magazine, a little handheld Garmin-45 filled the bill. Unfortunately, in the rush to get the boat ready, I had never gotten a chance to fool around with the thing. So, somewhere off New Bedford, I asked the crew if they wanted to play with the new toy.

Neither Larry nor Haydn had used a GPS before, but they were eager to give it a try. Within minutes they had mastered the instruction manual, entered our navigational waypoints throughout Buzzard's Bay into the thing's memory, turned on the widget's auto-guidance feature (keep the arrow pointed straight up and you are on course) and hit GOTO. BUCKRAMMER's navigation instantly entered the twenty-first century.

A Bang-Bang Day's End

BUCKRAMMER and her musketeers spent a pleasant early afternoon executing a number of looping tacks back and forth across Buzzard's Bay and playing with the GPS (accurate to about 15 feet, we found), noshing and lazing about as we did so. By 2:00 P.M. we approached the Cleveland Ledge Light tower and the entrance to the notorious Stony Point Dike section of the Cape Cod Canal, affectionately known to the locals as "The Spits."

When first opened in the early twentieth century, so the story goes, the western side of the canal veered almost a mile closer to the Cape Cod side of Buzzard's Bay. However, the hydrodynamics of this configuration caused excessive silting and the formation of bizarre currents and whirlpools. To remedy the situation, the Army Corps of Engineers dredged a new, more westerly canal section and lined it with over a mile of massive granite blocks (i.e., the dike). This so-called "new canal" solved the shoaling and current problem but created a new conundrum of its own in the form of tide-generated standing waves big enough to menace small craft. Whenever the tide flows out and wind flows in from the southwest, a mile-long, constantly breaking train of waves surfaces, making the Stony Point Dike area a no-man's-land for small boats.

I learned of this phenomenon the hard way in my youth. My father, brothers, friends and I had spent the day scuba diving from our *very* seaworthy, ex-Navy whaleboat DIVERSION near Bird Island, south of the Dike. On our way to the dive site, we had enjoyed an outgoing wind and tide with mirror-smooth seas. After our dive, the winds gradually began to shift around to the southwest. Not suspecting anything, we enjoyed a leisurely lunch before deciding to head back. DIVERSION arrived at the southern end of the Dike just in time for the southwesterlies to really blow up and the standing wave to form.

Imagine sailing along in calm seas one moment and the next moment finding yourself in a mile's worth of rapids, with 6- to 10-foot breakers; now picture shooting this torrent in a 26-foot, wide-open boat with eight adults and 1,600 pounds of scuba gear. I was scared from my topknot to my tailbone.

It took every trick we could muster to keep the little boat from broaching or swamping. Upon descending one particularly steep breaker, the bow of the whaleboat submerged and scooped up a few hundred gallons of Atlantic. (Think of the illustration depicting the "start of a pitchpole" in *Chapman Piloting*, the famous book on seamanship.) My father, sitting up in the bow, disappeared from view as the green sea engulfed him. When the boat finally recovered, Dad was nowhere to be found. For a moment we all feared the worst until his head popped up from behind the engine-bilge bulkhead, into which he had been washed. "I'm OK," he reported, "just a bit dinged."

After a white-knuckled hour of slugging along, DIVERSION finally cruised through the danger zone and into calm waters. I made a mental note to avoid this piece of ocean every chance that I could.

Now BUCKRAMMER's current tack would take us right through the heart of The Spits. Fortunately, the wind and sea were in harmony—at least for the sixty-minute window that remained open to us. After that, the current would turn and The Spits would once again serve up the chop for which they have earned their ill repute.

"Sorry to break the reverie, guys, but I think we've got a weather situation brewing." Haydn pointed astern, and Larry and I snapped our heads around to port. About 10 miles distant, the skies had darkened to greenish black, as sure a sign as any that one *mother* of a squall was about to spring upon us.

"*Shi*take mushrooms! Where the hell did that come from?"

Quick as a flash we broke out the foul-weather gear and began to prepare our little vessel for the blow.

I barked, "Everyone keep an eye on that water tower about three miles off in the distance. When it disappears into the storm it means we've got about five minutes before the squall hits." Experience has taught me that bad weather in Buzzard's Bay can close in at breathtaking speeds, often on the order of 45 mph. Large, distant objects in the storm's path, such as smokestacks or water towers, make good early warning indicators.

"There goes the tower," Larry yelled. As we watched, the water tower disappeared into the gloom.

In short order, the slickered crew scampered about BUCK-RAMMER, furling and gasketting the sail, stowing all loose items below decks, dogging the portholes, buttoning up the skylight and starting and engaging the engine.

A bit winded by the activities, Haydn finally called out, "All's set Cap!" Larry nodded in agreement and gave a thumbs-up just as the first heavy raindrops and lightning flashes made the squall's presence known. In a matter of seconds the wind swung around into the southwest and rose to 25 knots or so. Even though this wind direction still matched the heading of the canal's current, the seas began to build from a light chop to a breaker-infested, 4-foot following sea.

Large following seas are the nemesis of most boats but prove especially effective against catboats. The oversized, low-slung cockpit of the catboat provides a gigantic scoop for breaking green water. Even with self-draining scuppers, "many's the cat" swamped by a thousand-gallon swipe from behind.

Under normal conditions, we would allow BUCKRAMMER to weather the blow by coming about bow first into the wind and seas until the squall had passed. (Squalls usually pass in less than an hour.) However, I dared not risk having the current turn while we were hove to in the Stony Point Dike part of the canal. Considering that we already had 4-footers with all of nature flowing in the same direction, I couldn't imagine how bad this place would become once wind and water began to fight one another. I adjusted the throttle to better match the speed of the waves and asked Haydn and Larry to keep an eye out for rogue breakers sneaking up from behind. BUCKRAMMER's new-old engine responded to the settings and pushed us along.

The squall continued to intensify with increasing thunder and lightning and pelting hail and rain as we crept through the center of the Spits. Softly Larry whispered, "Gawd this is fun!"

Haydn and I looked at him and each other and broke into wide smiles. This *was* fun: great, amazing, exhilarating, straight-to-the-center-of-your-bones, gawd-damned, incredible fun. Boating offers a wide range of experiences, but some of the most memorable occur when everything works under trying conditions. Here we were on one of the most infamous stretches of water on the New England coast, in a wooden boat almost 100 years old, in gale-force winds, with sheets of rain and a jillion volts in the air. Yet we were dry, warm and in control. Wonderful stuff!

For the next hour, during the building fury of the blow, BUCKRAMMER and her custodians slugged along the Dike. A few breakers threatened and a couple of gusts gave us a zing or two, but the fun continued. Soon we had a mile or less to go before we could bear to port and into the safe haven of Onset Harbor. None of us noticed that the needle of the engine's water temperature gauge had crept into the danger zone and was now pegged against the pin on the right.

"Hey, does anyone smell anything?" I was the first to notice the characteristic rubbery, burnt-water odor. We all did and we all turned toward the temperature meter.

"Damn."

Just then Red, Jr. began to lose engine rpms, a potential sign of an overheated diesel in an engine-seizing death throe. Suddenly the thrilling conditions had turned threatening. Without an engine to power us along, the wind, the seas, the tides—everything would conspire to cause us harm.

The engine rpms continued to decline, and the exhaust smoke began to turn sooty. My first thought was that we had picked up some foreign object on our prop. Anything from eelgrass to lobster pot line could and sometimes did find the shaft a convenient place to wrap itself. The little Westerbeke 4-60 had enough trouble propelling five and a half tons of old wooden boat around. The burden of pushing the boat while acting as a rope or weed blender could stop things cold.

I slipped the engine out of gear for a moment. If we had snagged something, this would quickly unload the system and the engine rpms would return to normal. In this case, a quick burst of reverse thrust would often unfoul things and restore order.

The engine continued to sputter to the point that it became harder and harder to maintain helm control. If the engine died under the present conditions, the boat would come about and point up into the wind. For a minute or so, while this happened, BUCKRAMMER would lie beam-to the seas and become a prime candidate for a boat-flipping broach.

"Blast." The failure of the "out-of-gear" test meant that something more fundamental was at work. The weather continued to worsen.

I told Hayden to take the wheel and went to the front of the binnacle and removed the engine cover. What the heck could be doing this? My mind raced through a dozen possibilities as I scanned the now-exposed red engine. A blown cooling hose could have this effect, but we would have seen billows of steam. Suddenly I noticed that the water intake filter was green. This fist-sized plastic gadget connects to the ocean on one end and to the engine's water pump on the other end. It looks like a jelly jar with a piece of window screen inside. In operation, the Westerbeke's water pump pulls cold seawater through the filter. The internal screen stops any foreign matter, from seaweed to jellyfish, from entering and damaging the water pump. Normally the filter is filled with clean seawater and looks transparent. Now it appeared to be filled with a green, paint-like substance that clearly blocked cooling water from reaching the engine. What to do?

One of BUCKRAMMER's previous owners had the foresight to install a seawater bypass on the water pump. A flip of a lever would cause cooling water to be drawn from the bilge instead of the ocean. This setup allows the engine to be used as a bilge pump in case of emergencies. I looked into the bilge and, as usual, saw a few gallons of water swishing around. BUCKRAMMER, like many cats her age, has a "wet bilge" due to factors ranging from minor leaks below the waterline to rainwater leaks from above. By flipping the lever, bilge water would be slurped into the cooling system. This would hopefully lower the engine temperature and buy me a few seconds to open the filter and unclog the darned thing.

Larry had watched over my shoulder throughout the thirty seconds or so it had taken me to remove the engine cover and assess the situation. I explained what I was about to do, and with the confidence of a neurosurgeon he replied, "Worth a shot. What the hell?"

The lever flipped, BUCKRAMMER now ran on bilge water cooling. Within ten seconds Haydn reported that the engine rpms had stabilized and that the temperature gauge needle had twitched to the left of the red pin. Larry and I quickly unscrewed the filter and found the screen blocked by a piece of green, trash-bag plastic. "Sonofagun! You never know what's sailing on the high seas these days!"

We cleared the plastic sheet, reassembled the filter and flipped the intake lever to the ocean setting. Glorious, cool, clean Atlantic Ocean water surged through the filter, into the water pump and through the engine's heat exchanger and exhaust. The engine's temperature rapidly returned to the "green" zone and Red, Jr., in turn, returned to its old but vigorous self.

Haydn gunned the throttle and we shot through the tail end of The Spits in record time. Soon we found ourselves in the protected calm of the approach channel to Onset Bay— and not a moment too soon. Behind us in the canal, the tide had turned and a nightmarish 12-foot, comber-filled sea had risen.

Larry let out a low whistle. "Now *that* would not have been fun."

Onset Dalliance

Onset Bay in Wareham, Massachusetts provides mariners with a wonderful, old-fashioned place to unwind on the western end of the land-cut portion of the Cape Cod Canal. It offers warm, clean waters with good holding ground and all manner of marine services. After a daylong, adventure-filled sail, Onset provided the perfect setting for a quiet evening.

We hailed the dockmaster of the Point Independence

Yacht Club on VHF channel 9. A few minutes later and $20 lighter, we secured BUCKRAMMER to one of his club's guest moorings and made things shipshape. In my impoverished youth, I would not have even considered paying for an overnight mooring. Middle age, however, had softened my resistance. Hot showers, club facilities such as swimming pools and tennis courts, home-cooked food and, er, professional beverage services all proved to be siren songs enough to justify the twenty bucks. In the present case, it also helped that Larry and Haydn offered to pay. My gray-haired days had also made me comfortable with the expression, "Sure! That's mighty generous of you guys."

We rowed to the club's dock, hit the showers and spruced ourselves up. The PIYC was hosting one of their famous "fish fry" buffets, and that sounded pretty good to us all. We enjoyed a wonderful meal and followed it with a walk into Onset Village for a hand-dipped ice cream cone. A little while after sunset, we rowed back to the boat and, in short order, slipped under the covers and began sawing wood.

Morning seemed to arrive especially early but, grogginess aside, in no time we had the griddle fired up, blueberry pancakes on the table and French roast in the mugs. As we dabbed up the last licks of syrup, Leo and Deb Donahue appeared on the yacht club's main dock and waved us hello.

I fired up Red, Jr., Larry untied the mooring line and we motored over to pick up our fourth musketeer. Neither of the Donahues had ever seen BUCKRAMMER in the flesh before and I was not sure how they would react. Deb's sister is married to Ned Benjamin, co-owner of the world famous Gannon and Benjamin boatyard on Martha's Vineyard, builders and restorers of some of the most incredible wooden vessels afloat. As a result, the Donahues are used to first-rate small craft and best-of-breed craftsmanship. From a distance my old boat looks, arguably, magnificent. Up close and personal, she shows her true workboat pedigree. As BUCKRAMMER nestled up against the dock, I could feel Deb and Leo eyeing the boat.

"Good morning," I chirped. "Soooo. Whadayathink?"

The Donahues looked at me, looked at the crew, and looked at one another. Deb spoke first.

"Interesting!"

Leo quickly chimed in. "Yes! Very authentic." After a moment of awkward silence, we all burst into laughter.

"OK, Mr. Conway," Leo offered. "Let's get the show on the road."

We quickly topped off the boat's fuel tank, bid farewell to Deb and headed out toward the western entrance of the canal. If all went according to plan, the boatload of us would motor through the canal (the Army Corps of Engineers forbid sailing in the canal), enter Cape Cod Bay and then head due north following the 18-fathom curve along the coast. To continue our gentlemanly approach to this cruise, BUCKRAMMER would put into Scituate Harbor instead of killing herself to reach Boston. Scituate lies about 20 miles south of the city and offers a spectacular port of call. Even better, the Donahues maintained a summer cottage there and offered us full use of it, showers and real beds included.

As previously mentioned, the Cape Cod Canal produces a wicked current. As a result, the Army Corps discourages "against the flow" travel through the land cut. So on any given day, a large number of small craft (and VERY LARGE craft as well) will "stage up" on either the eastern or western end awaiting the turning of the tide. To determine when the transit window opens, mariners turn to the "yellow book" otherwise known as the *Eldridge Tide and Pilot Book*. For this morning, *Eldridge* forecast a 9:30 A.M. beginning to the west-to-east flow. The time was now 8:00 A.M.; given Onset's proximity to the canal, we would easily be in position by 8:30 or so to stage up and then shoot through.

BUCKRAMMER quickly put Wareham behind her and headed toward the waiting area. As we rounded Onset Island, we noticed that a remarkably large, three- or four-masted, square-rigged ship had put into the joint Mass Maritime Academy/Army Corps docks near the mouth of the canal. Haydn pulled out our guide to the Sail Boston 2000 event and quickly identified the great ship as the four-masted bark KRUZENSHTERN out of Kaliningrad, our first tall ship of the cruise.

"Let's get closer." Leo was the first to say what we all were thinking. The Army Corps' dock and the KRUZENSHTERN were both within the approved turn-of-the-tide waiting zone, so I pointed BUCKRAMMER in that direction and nudged her engine's throttle up a tad. As we closed in on the ship, our mouths drooped an ever-increasing amount. The thing was gigantic! At 346 feet, the KRUZENSHTERN was almost half the length of the TITANIC. Beside her, BUCKRAMMER dwindled to lifeboat size, but we were in good company. A small flotilla of pleasure boats circled alongside the Russian vessel, and even the 60-odd-foot Egg Harbor cabin cruiser just ahead of us looked minuscule in comparison.

A number of Russian sailors lined their ship's rail, surveying the scene and waving to the pretty girls on the toy boats below. No one waved to us, until . . .

"Voud small boot vid big sail please to bord?" A booming voice fell on us from aloft. "Voud small boot please to bord?"

We four musketeers looked at one another with a common "what the hell is that all about" look. Suddenly, an American-accented voice came over the speaker.

"You jokers in the old catboat: Bring that tub over to the dock, on the double."

None of us saw anyone but I gestured and pointed to myself as if to acknowledge this voice-of-God-like command.

"That's right buddy, you in the white shirt and your three buddies. Now!"

With that I spun BUCKRAMMER about, navigated around the KRUZENSHTERN and came alongside the quay. A few Corps staffers grabbed our lines, made us fast and commanded us to wait there.

Haydn whispered in my ear, "All right Cap, what did we do wrong?"

"Beats me."

A few minutes passed with no activity. Then, on the gangplank of the KRUZENSHTERN, we noticed a small party of about five individuals rapidly descending in our direction. Three of them wore the largest-rimmed officer's caps that I have ever seen. They raced along the dock and soon stood next to BUCKRAMMER's cockpit. The officer with the largest hat and the most medals and fruit salad thrust out a massive paw.

"Kepp Codd Catboot! Kepp Codd Catboot! Pleased to cum-board? Da?"

I extended my hand over BUCKRAMMER's coaming, placed it into the Russian's vise grip and shook aggressively. In rapid succession the rest of BUCKRAMMER's gang did likewise. By this time a few, official-looking Americans had caught up with the situation. The most senior of these explained.

"Hey Cap! Ivan here and his boys got all excited when they saw your sailboat. His brother owns a fiberglass one of these things on a lake somewhere in northern Italy. Seems like his bro asked him to seek out an authentic example of the original class. How old is this thing?"

Still dumbfounded, I replied, "Built in 1908."

The Russian without the hat (we'll call him "No Hat") quickly translated for the Big Hatted bloke.

"Da! Da!"

The American cast me a glance. "Guess she'll do. OK then, I respectfully request permission for our party to come aboard."

"Granted!"

In a flash the whole shore party jumped into our cockpit. Larry, Leo, Haydn and I were quickly relegated to the status of tour guides on our own vessel. For the next thirty minutes Big Hat poked, prodded and examined BUCKRAMMER's every nook and cranny all the while asking No Hat questions in the mother tongue. No Hat, in turn, translated the questions into relatively good English, to which we replied. In this manner we educated our new comrades as to the who's, what's, when's, where's, why's and how's of early-twentieth-century catboats. Everyone (including the Americans!) had his or her turn at the wheel for a photo op. When the visitors had satisfied their catboat lusts, they disembarked and once again stood abeam of our boat on the dock. Big Hat turned and spoke.

"You now come ship ours now? Da?"

The musketeers all shrugged in confusion. The senior American chided us.

"You lugs have just been invited aboard the KRUZEN-SHTERN. I suggest that you quickly accept."

I gave Big Hat my widest smile. "Da! Da! Da!"

And that is how four catboat "lugs" found themselves guests of the Motherland aboard one of her finest sail-training ships. Over the next hour or so, Big Hat and his associates gave us the $10 tour of the KRUZENSHTERN. From our examination we learned:

- The masts of the big ship, towering 185 feet above deck level, had proven too tall for 135-foot clearance of the three bridges that span the canal. So KRUZEN-SHTERN would enjoy the hospitality of the Army Corps while awaiting approval for her new, "long way around" course to Boston (south through Buzzard's Bay, east beneath Nantucket Island and northeast past Cape Cod).
- The K-ship is the very last of a German-owned and operated fleet of ships known as the Flying-P Liners. She and her sisters carried grain from around the world to Hamburg in the early part of the twentieth century.
- Much like our own U.S. Coast Guard ship EAGLE, "Das Kruz" was awarded to the Russians as a "gift" following World War II. Also like our EAGLE, she serves as a training ship for naval cadets.

- She "hosts" about 68 crew and 110 cadets and provides them all with bed linens and *four* square meals a day while underway.

During the course of our inspection, we happened across the officer's mess right in the middle of one of these four meals. In high-speed Russian, Big Hat's No-Hatted associate explained to those gathered in the mess who we were and what we were about. Upon hearing this an officer in the mess came over to us and, in perfect English, said: "Welcome comrades! Join us for brunch. We are having American cornflakes. We *love* American cornflakes!"

As he spoke a steward set up four bowls on the table in front of us. In a flash a heaping portion of Kellogg's best were poured into each bowl. Then, while a pitcher of milk was placed on the table, another steward gave each of us a coffee cup filled with "water."

Haydn turned to me and said, "I get the cornflakes and milk part, but where does the 'water' figure in?"

Leo gave me a poke and pointed to an officer one table removed from ours. As we watched, the officer emptied his "water"-filled mug over the cornflakes. He then took the milk pitcher and, tipping it over ever so slightly, splashed about a tablespoon of milk into the bowl.

From the corner of his mouth Larry commented, "No wonder they love American cornflakes. Given that much 'water', even beach sand would taste pretty good."

Big Hat smiled. "Journ us."

Who were we to argue? Son of a gun, a body could get used to this "water"-drenched American staple.

A Northerly Slugfest

After "brunch" we bid farewell to our Russian hosts, reboarded BUCKRAMMER and pushed out into the now easterly flowing current of the Cape Cod Canal. It was coming up on 10:45 A.M., which meant that we'd have to hustle to reach Scituate in time for dinner. Fortunately, the forecast of a beam-reaching "15-knot southwesterly with a light chop in Cape Cod Bay" promised fast sailing on our way north.

Red, Jr., with a boost from the easterly moving current, pushed our woodpile along through the canal at a delightful 10 knots ground speed. We quickly passed under the Railroad, Bourne and Sagamore Bridges—not a problem for our 32-foot mast.

Haydn Samuel and I are rabid fans of the National Public Radio show *Car Talk*—in the metro-Boston area, Saturday at 11:00 A.M. means *Car Talk*. In our planning for the trip I had assured Haydn that within BUCKRAMMER's "kit," he would find a radio suitable for receiving the show. With show time rapidly approaching, I went below to dig through the duffle bags to find the radio. I had just found it when Leo and Larry came down into the cabin. Both looked serious.

"We're almost out of the canal and you'd better come up on deck," Larry said.

Leo added, "Yeah, looks like we're about to hit the proverbial fan up ahead."

I bolted up into the cockpit. Up ahead, at the mouth of the canal, the sea seethed and boiled. From this distance it looked like a standing wave with 3- to 4-foot breakers. Leo told me that most of the boats that had accompanied us through the canal, upon seeing what lay ahead, had diverted into the East-End Marina now about 300 yards astern. The intensity of the canal current would make it hard to come about and dash back into the marina, so it looked like we were in for a bit of action.

I yelled, "Prepare for battle stations everyone." Without a word the musketeers sprung into action, rapidly gathering and stowing all loose items while battening all else down. Once again, BUCKRAMMER was about to make an instantaneous transition from tranquility to trauma. As is standard policy in rough going, all aboard donned life jackets. This way, worst case, only the insurance company would get hurt if anything bad happened.

As we approached the tumult it became clear that Bucky was about to joust with 6- to 8-footers, not the smaller waves that we thought we observed from an eighth of a mile back.

"Hold on!"

The boat entered the boil at a 30-degree angle and immediately took green water over the bows and cabin top. The wind had shifted into a head-on, northeasterly direction that blew the spray smack into the cockpit. We all got soaked. BUCKRAMMER's five and a half tons shook off the first assault, raced down the back of the wave, recovered and met the next breaker. Sploosh! Another few hundred gallons of Cape Cod Bay smacked our old boat's nose and saturated her crew. This experience began to take on the unsettling aspects of my long-ago experience in The Spits. This time, however, I was not in an open boat but rather in a covered vessel with the reputation of being "tight as a tick" in conditions such as these. While a bit shaken, the boat handled herself remarkably well, all things considered.

"Imagine the bouncing we'd be getting if this were a lightweight fiberglass boat," Larry commented. "We'd be all over creation." That thought, while comforting, did not cause me to relax my grip on the boat's wheel or make my white knuckles any pinker. We still had a long slugfest ahead and with a vessel as old as ours other factors, such as sprung planks and touchy engine fuel-stop springs, sometimes outweigh seakindly mass.

Haydn gripped my shoulder. "Mind that buoy, eh?"

I quickly looked to starboard. Somehow the current was pushing us forward and to starboard, both at great speed. Without a rapid course change, BUCKRAMMER would collide with a massive channel marker zooming up on us. I tried to compensate by turning the wheel to port but the effect was negligible. The buoy was almost upon us. With seconds to spare, I pushed Red, Jr.'s throttle to the maximum position. Our heading changed only slightly but we sideslipped enough to put the buoy about 10 feet off our rail as we shot past.

The increased speed gave us better helm control but pushed the old boat's bow deeper into the breakers. With no further buoys in sight, I eased the throttle back to a less bone-crunching position. What a freaking ride!

A waterlogged Leo stepped back to the helm station. "What do you think is causing these waves, and how long will they last?"

"Clearly there's some interaction between the canal current flowing out into Cape Cod Bay and the wind-generated seas coming in," I replied. "I'm hoping that once we're out of the mainstream of the canal things will improve dramatically." Leo just grimaced.

Fact was, these conditions should not have existed had the weather forecast been correct. Strong northeast winds were not in the plan, yet the slap-in-our-face, driven spray said otherwise.

I continued. "This eastern end of the canal is bounded by a man-made breakwater to the north and extensive foul grounds to the south. We're currently smack dab in the bottleneck created by these two formations. In about a mile or so we'll be past the breakwater and able to turn to port and north. At that point, assuming the onshore winds continue, we'll only have to contend with wind-generated waves and not the deadly duo of the waves fighting against the current." This seemed to satisfy Leo and it made me feel a bit better as well.

After a brutal ten minutes, the breakwater finally ended and we turned and set course for Scituate. Once out of the current, we also left the nastiest sections of the standing wave behind. Unfortunately the northeast wind continued, producing a white-capped sea now directly on our beam.

Larry held up our handheld VHF radio and gestured at the speaker. "Not to worry, John. NOAA says we should experience gentle, offshore winds from here to Maine." Haydn, upset that these unpredicted conditions had caused him to miss *Car Talk*, just scowled. "Maybe those government chuckleheads have their compass turned upside down."

Maybe they did, for over the next hour the northeast winds freshened to 20 to 25 knots, with gale-force gusts and 4-foot, breaking seas. The gentle southwesterlies were nowhere to be found. In these conditions we decided to leave BUCKRAMMER's sail tightly furled and gasketted. This was a big disappointment for all aboard—we are sailors after all, not stinkpotters—but discretion was, in this instance, definitely the better part of valor.

Between the Cape Cod Canal and the North River (just south of Scituate) is one of the most boring stretches of coast around Boston. Only two ports of refuge, Plymouth Harbor and Green Harbor, punctuate miles and miles of empty beach.

Plymouth Harbor you ask? *The* Plymouth Harbor? Yes, *the* Plymouth Harbor of Pilgrim fame provides one of the diversions. The problem with Plymouth is both its distance from the shipping lane and the trickiness of the approach. From where we were, BUCKRAMMER could be snug on a mooring in Scituate in the same time it would take her to navigate the miles of serpentine, mudflat-riddled channels that lead to Plymouth.

In contrast, Green Harbor is just an oversized guzzle tucked into the marshes behind the community of Brant Rock. Unfortunately this potential refuge has a number of strikes against it. First, it presents one of the most rock-infested approaches on the New England coast. Second, it has served as the biting, stinging and sucking bug capital of South Shore Massachusetts for as long as anyone can remember. Finally, shoreside amenities are few and far between. At least for this journey, these factors took Green Harbor off the list. So it was Scituate or bust!

In an odd way, BUCKRAMMER and her new, old Westerbeke seemed in harmony with Nature's unforecast sea state.

The occasional rogue breaker would bite us now and then, and the internal organs of the captain and crew were stressed in heretofore-unimagined ways by the body-slamming conditions. Yet our whole, little menagerie somehow continued to move north slowly.

Six hours from the Cape Cod Canal, we finally passed Scituate Light and crossed into the relative calm of her harbor. To a man, the musketeers let out a sigh. We all longed mightily for dry clothes, a hot meal and cold beers.

In my book, Scituate is a perfect harbor for a sailor cruising the New England coast. From her deepwater channels and extensive marine facilities to her proximity to grocery and hardware stores, restaurants and movie theaters, this IS the place. On passing the Scituate Harbor Yacht Club, we radioed one of several marinas and inquired about overnight moorings. For the traditional $20 per night we booked an anchorage that included twenty-four-hour motorized tender service, a security patrol, freshwater showers and the newspaper of our choice delivered with coffee for all aboard in the morning. Not too bad!

As we pulled up to our designated mooring buoy, Larry once again consulted the handheld VHF. "Hey everyone! The NOAA weather forecast has changed. It now says that small craft warnings will be flying from this morning to this evening. Seems a few hours late, eh?" The rest of the musketeers just smiled and shook their heads.

As the tender took us ashore, Leo cell-phoned his better half and asked her to come and get us. By the time we reached the dock, Deb had arrived with her SUV. We all climbed aboard and in no time were showered, shaved and shipshape, enjoying the overnight hospitality of the Donahue clan.

Sunday began with a lumberjack breakfast at one of Scituate's local diners. After slipping our belts a notch or two and buying a few essentials (a new boathook and some transmission oil for Red, Jr.), we headed back to BUCKRAM-

MER and made ready for the last leg of our journey to Bean-town.

The weather remained sunny and warm but the wind and seas had dropped to dead calm. NOAA weather continued to post small craft warnings, but the actual conditions would have been suitable for sailing in a dugout canoe.

With no wind to speak of we once again counted on Red, Jr. to work its magic. We sailor types were once more disappointed and lamented that we had used more of the cast-iron breeze on this trip thus far than the real thing. The sight of the city of Boston in the distance tempered this, however. We were almost there.

The infamous Minot's Light, Cohasset, Nantasket Beach and the treacherous Hardings Ledge passed by during our three-hour morning cruise. Shortly before noon, BUCKRAMMER passed Little Brewster Island and the legendary Boston Light. We had arrived.

BUCKRAMMER passes historic Boston Light and enters the outer harbor. (L/R) with the "Three Musketeers"; Leo Donahue, Haydn Samuel and (at the wheel) Larry Borges.

The Smell of Boston in the Morning

What few boating skills I possess were honed during my college years through time spent on, in and under Boston's inner and outer harbor waters. This remarkable archipelago of nearly thirty islands offers mariners an extraordinary and unlimited collection of experiences. Deepwater channels, swirling, ever-changing winds, haunted castles, secret fortresses, shipwrecks, treasure, untouched Nature and much, much more all await the boater in the shadow of Boston.

Life's little quirks had kept me away from these waters for almost twenty years. Yet as BUCKRAMMER transited the Brewster Islands, the unmistakable smell of salt air mixed with a million big city fragrances triggered some primal response that shouted Boston Harbor. I never realized until that moment how profound and lasting an impact the few years I had spent here had made. Remarkable! Haydn broke the reverie.

"Hey lover boy. You look like someone who has just entered Nirvana rather than the Boston ship channel. Are you OK?"

"Er, sure!" I replied.

"All right then," Haydn continued. "So I suppose you'll be want'n to check out the big boy ahead of us, eh?"

I turned my noggin and spied a good-sized, totally white, square-rigged ship directly ahead. Leo grabbed the binoculars, took a glance and said, "She's the PICTON CASTLE out of Lunenburg. Ever hear of her?"

"Yes sir! She's a metal-hulled former steamer converted to sail a few years ago. She circumnavigates the globe on a regular basis, manned mostly by greenhorns seeking a hands-on, tall-ship experience. Very cool."

Not bad! I thought. Less than an hour in Boston waters and we had already sighted one of the other Sail Boston 2000 participants. Haydn took the wheel and increased our

speed to catch up with "The Castle." Within a few minutes
we were broadside to the steel beauty. I cupped my hands
to my mouth and yelled across to her helmsman, "What ship
and whither?"

He boomed back, "We're the PICTON CASTLE, two days out
of New York and bound for Hull Gut. What boat are you?"

I yelled back, "We be the BUCKRAMMER, three days out of
Westport Point and Boston bound."

The PICTON's helmsman saluted as we dropped back into
her wake.

Each vessel participating in the Sail Boston 2000 event
had been assigned an anchorage location or a berth courtesy
of a sponsoring yacht club depending on her size and needs.
The Hull Yacht Club had volunteered to host the splendifer-
ous catboat fleet. Weeks prior to the event Catboat Association President Bob Luckraft had asked that we rendezvous at
the club no later than 7:00 that evening to meet and greet

Larry Borges sights our first tall ship, the PICTON CASTLE.

our sponsors. This meant that we now had almost five hours to kill.

I called everyone to order and asked, "What say we have a little lunch and check out the harbor?" Food being the wonderful motivator that it is, not a single musketeer argued for an alternative course of action. With a cry of, "The deli is open for business, boys!" Haydn climbed into the galley, dug out the ham, turkey, rye bread, onions, pickles, chips, mayo, mustard, tomatoes and lettuce and took sandwich orders. Leo brought the ice chest up from below into the cockpit and handed everyone the cold drink of his choice. In the midst of all of this food and drink flying about, the wind suddenly picked up from the friendly southwest.

"Let's go sailing!"

I ran forward, ungasketted the sail, ran back into the cockpit, killed the engine and hoisted the halyards. BUCK-RAMMER spread her wing and *sailed* into the outer harbor, in proper catboat fashion, while we slurped cold ones and ate Dagwood sandwiches.

A Flag of a Different Color

For the remainder of Sunday and throughout most of Monday, BUCKRAMMER and her intrepid crew sailed around and about coastal Boston. The weather remained picture perfect as we explored the nooks and crannies of the Boston waterfront and visited the CONSTITUTION ("Old Ironsides"), the nuclear-powered carrier ENTERPRISE, the JFK Memorial Library, Logan Airport, Fort Warren on George's Island, Fort Independence on Castle Island and the Nix's Mate pyramid, where colonial Boston hung captured pirates out to dry (and die). On Sunday evening we made it back to the Hull Yacht Club in time to meet up with the rest of the Catboat Association gang. The yacht club members welcomed us with open arms and placed the entire club at our disposal. They also organized a tour of the restored Hull Lifesavers Station (precursor to the U.S. Coast Guard), held a grand cookout and allowed BUCKRAMMER to dock for the duration on the club's main float. In many ways we felt more at home with these wonderful people than if we had been in our own homeports.

During the Sunday evening barbecue, Luckraft explained the process by which we would join and participate in the Grand Parade of Sail on Tuesday morning. The Association had been given a number of orange-colored pennant flags imprinted with the Sail Boston 2000 logo. Attached to the forestays of our boats, the flags would signal the Coast Guard patrol boats that we were legitimate parade participants. On Tuesday morning, we would head out to the assembly area near Deer Island Light. From there, parade organizers would assign us a position in the procession. Sometime around 9:00 A.M. on Tuesday, Old Ironsides would leave her berth at the Charlestown Navy Yard, deep within the inner harbor. By 10:00 A.M. she would reach Deer Island Light, fire a cannon or two, come about and lead the line of small craft and tall ships back into Boston. Parade officials had said that the small craft, represented both by the old catboats and by a number of equally old Friendship sloops, would fall into place behind Old Ironsides, ahead of the "Big Boys." When the small craft had reached the CONSTITUTION's pier, they would peel off and head back out to their host clubs while the large ships would dock along the immediate Boston waterfront for public boarding. It all sounded grand.

Parade Day dawned sunny, warm *and early!* A few new guests, including my daughter Abby, Leo's daughter Meg and the crew of a Friendship sloop that had lost her rudder, all boarded BUCKRAMMER around 6:00 A.M. so that we could leave in plenty of time to reach the staging area. We attached the orange "participant" pennant to the most visible part of the forestay. At 6:30 A.M. all of the catboats participating in the event bid farewell to our Hull hosts and began the 5-mile journey to Deer Island. In short order both the PICTON CAS-

TLE and the graceful clipper, PRIDE OF BALTIMORE II, both of which had been anchored behind Pendleton Island near Hull Gut, joined our flotilla.

"Hey Captain! Do you need a pumpout?" On the way, just off of George's Island, a Sail Boston 2000 "official septic discharge" vessel hailed us.

Quizzically I yelled back, "Not right now, but thanks anyway." As we watched, he made the same offer to each of the other catboats in the group.

Abby joined me at the wheel. "Hey Dad, I think our old bucket has just been heckled by a sewer pumper. The nerve!" I agreed, but was not about to let a wise-guy septic professional ruin the moment.

The catboats proceeded through the channel between George's and Rainsford Islands, past Nix's Mate and toward the gathering sailing fleet. As we neared Long Island Light, diagonally across from Deer Island, yet another septic boat pulled up alongside and asked us to hove to "for a flush."

The PRIDE OF BALTIMORE II overtakes, and almost skewers, BUCKRAMMER off Hull.

Again I just waved him off. He shrugged, made the same offer to the other cats and, rebuked by them as well, motored off to pester some other boaters. The nerve indeed.

About a quarter mile from our destination, a Coast Guard patrol crew spied the catboat collection, put their boat into overdrive and screamed up into our midst. A burly, officer type held a megaphone to his face and barked, "Sorry gentlemen, this area is off-limits to all but parade participants under Temporary Regulation DOCID:Fr15. Please come about and clear the zone."

Simultaneously, all of the catboat skippers bolted from their cockpits, raced forward and pointed to their respective orange participant flags. Nonplussed, the officer once again hit the talk button on his bullhorn.

"For the last time, gentlemen, this area is off-limits to all but parade participants under Temporary Regulation DOCID:Fr15mr00-18. Please come about and clear the zone or you will be fined."

A crew member on one of the catboats produced a bullhorn as well and replied, "Officer! We understand your directive but all of us are participants in the parade. Please notice the parade pennants affixed to our forestays and allow us to pass."

The Guardsmen caucused among themselves. The officer boomed back. "Gentlemen, we do not recognize the Sail Boston 2000 Septic Pumpout Request pennant as admission to the Grand Parade of Sail. Please hove to and have your chief representative hail us on VHF 72 for further direction."

Seven sets of hands grabbed for BUCKRAMMER's marine radio and set the dial for channel 72. In a three-way conversation with Luckraft and the officer we ascertained that the Catboat Association had been issued the wrong (WAY WRONG) set of pennants for the event. This was hammered home when yet a third pumpout boat pulled up into our midst and asked if they could be of service.

Needless to say, with our existing pennant we were

hosed under good old DOCID:Fr15mr00-18. Hosed! And in more ways than one. No flag, no parade!

The musketeers, fire in their eyes, girded for battle. Then we collectively placed our tails between our legs and signaled to the Coast Guard that we would comply. As my father once said, "Never argue with anyone carrying a bigger gun than you." This was, after all, pleasure boating.

The Catboat Association members rafted together to discuss what to do. After a whole pile of language, everyone agreed that the group had not come all this way just to miss the Grand Parade—even if it meant that we would be relegated to spectator status. So one by one, the members motored over into the approved observation areas and anchored in.

BUCKRAMMER and the author head back to Westport from Hull Bay.

Right on schedule, Old Ironsides fired her guns and officially began the show. From our ringside seats we enjoyed a spectacular view of this once-in-a-lifetime event. As the last of the huge vessels passed, sometime around 2:00 P.M., our pride had recovered to the point that life on the high seas was once again something wonderful, majestic and inspiring.

Epilogue

We never *did* receive a satisfactory explanation for what went wrong. Officials of Sail Boston 2000 assured us, however, that the Catboat Association would absolutely participate in the next event, if and when that occurs.

Meanwhile, after depositing the musketeers and other stragglers back on terra firma, I turned BUCKRAMMER south and *single-handedly* headed back toward Westport Point. But that, as they say in Tristan Jones novels, is another story.

5

—◦/◦/◦—

Treasure Hunters
of Brenton Cove

"It's mid-August and the summer's over, as far as I'm concerned."

Caroline, fresh back from camp and about to start a baby-sitting stint, folded her arms and scowled. Youngest of the three Conway kids at fourteen, she found herself an only child with her two older siblings just off to college early.

"Not so!" I shot back. "There's tons of summer left if you have the imagination and motivation to give it a go."

But after unsuccessfully exploring options ranging from Caroline camping out with her friends to my teaching her how to drive a stick shift, things began to look grim.

"Er, let's sleep on it," I suggested. As I drifted off that night, a fleeting thought passed through the old cranial, but it submerged just as quickly. "Nah! She'd never go for it."

Over English muffins the next morning I casually salvaged the previous night's big, bad idea. "How about a treasure hunt?"

"Huh?"

"A treasure hunt—you know, gold doubloons, pieces of eight, pirates flying the Jolly Roger and all that sort of thing."

"Daaaad . . . I think you're a few doughnuts shy of a dozen."

"No wait, hear me out. OK?"

A crack appeared in the teen's armor. "Well all right, I'm listening." The window of opportunity had opened and I stepped through.

The Quest Described

I explained that about thirty years ago I had attended a lecture given by New England diving legend Captain Brad Luther at a Sea Rover's Convention in Boston. Captain Luther's talk focused on the location and history of shipwrecks along the Rhode Island coast. One of these wrecks, located in Newport's Brenton Cove, just begged exploration. No one knew the history of the old ship and few had explored its resting place, but old Captain Luther was convinced that she would be a worthy dive. Best of all, the wreck had settled in only 12 to 15 feet of water, so explorers could easily probe its mysteries with only a face mask, snorkel and flippers. Finding it would also be easy, as it lay right at the base of a cliff just below a well-known Newport mansion.

"All of these years I have intended to validate the captain's tale but found neither the time nor the company. Of course, many years have passed and the darn thing may have broken up and melted away by now, but . . . what say we give it a go?"

Caroline squinted in a manner that showed active thought going on.

"Just you and me, say, over a weekend and I suppose on the old BUCKRAMMER?"

"Yeah! Something like that."

The squinting continued.

"And could we visit the Newport shops on Thames Avenue and only eat in restaurants?"

"If you use your own money in the shops and limit the restaurant visits to dinner," I countered.

"Hmmm. OK, you've got a deal, but only on a weekend that I'm not busy."

"Not busy! I thought that the whole idea was to find ways to *keep* busy?"

"Daaad!"

So it was off to fortune and glory: the girl, me and the catboat.

The Quest Begins

Our route would take us due south of Westport to the first waypoint, the wreck site of the pre–World War II Canadian "four-pipe" destroyer HMCS ST. FRANCIS. This former U.S. Navy tin can had been rammed and sunk while under tow for repairs in July of 1945. Salvage efforts in the 1950s had removed all but a large section of bow. Resting in 10 fathoms at 41°27'.42"N, 71°.06'.20"W, the bow portion serves as a reliable, if somewhat peculiar, aid to navigation by providing a wonderful double echo return on a depth-sounder—sound trapped inside the metal bow reverbs a second, so-called "ghost" echo. From the wreck, BUCKRAMMER would turn west and make a beeline for the Brenton Reef buoy and the notorious entrance to Narragansett Bay and Newport Harbor.

Fully provisioned for adventure, Caroline, the cat and I chugged out of Westport Harbor to fortune and glory. Before long, with Caroline at the wheel and BUCKRAMMER on a broad reach, we closed in on the ST. FRANCIS.

"Hey Dad! Hand me that fishing rod," Caroline commanded. "I bet that old wreck is crawling with game fish."

I slipped below, grabbed the tackle box, rod and reel, handed them to Caroline and took the helm.

"The old-timers say that this wreck attracts everything from bluefish to yellowfin tuna," I chimed in, rummaging in the tackle box. "So I'd suggest, hmmm, a *Rebel* lure." My expert selection was influenced by the fact that our tackle box held but one lure, that being a Rebel!

Caroline, eyeing me suspiciously, gingerly took the lure, snapped it onto the leader, executed a perfect cast off the stern and in no time had about 200 feet of fifty-pound test streaming over the transom. BUCKRAMMER sounded the wreck, spun over, turned into a controlled jibe and then headed toward Newport under a powder blue, crystal-clear sky. What a day!

Caroline and I settled into our respective routines, she trolling, casting and cranking, dislodging seaweed and then repeating the process, while I tweaked the sail, fooled around with my handheld GPS, diddled with the radio and adjusted the depth-sounder. BUCKRAMMER just sailed along, mostly staying on course.

Off Sakonnet Point, Caroline grabbed my arm. "How big do yellowfin tuna get?"

Caroline almost caught the fish of her life (or did it almost catch her?) on our way to Newport.

Awakened from my technological reveries, I replied, "I have no idea; a hundred pounds, I guess. Why?"

Pointing over the stern Caroline calmly answered, "Then I guess that's something else."

Peering over the transom, I nearly swallowed my tongue. Trailing behind us, just inches from our barn door rudder and only about 5 feet under the surface was the biggest "fish" I had ever seen. Seemingly oblivious to BUCKRAMMER, the monster silently cruised under our hull in the direction of our centerboard.

Bump!

The beast tapped the board and nudged BUCKRAMMER a few feet to starboard. Caroline and I jumped onto the cabin roof just in time to see the great fish transit our suddenly *very small* vessel.

Caroline whispered, "Holy cow! Using BUCKRAMMER as a measuring stick, I bet that thing is eighteen or twenty feet long."

"Twenty at least," I whispered back as the beast slinked off into the deep.

With no one at the helm, our old boat began to round up into the wind. I scooted to the wheel and put us back on course. Caroline still held her fishing rod with most of its line trailing behind the boat. She and I looked at one another and exchanged a psychic instant message. In less time than it takes to say "Call me Ishmael," the line, leader, lure and all were back on board.

"I think I'll give this fishing thing a rest for a while," she said.

Both of us burst into laughter, bid the monster adieu (we believe that it was a basking shark) and continued our westward journey.

A Wet Dry-Run

A little after 1:00 P.M., we passed the Brenton Reef buoy and altered course north by east into Narragansett Bay. The weather remained picture perfect with warm, offshore winds of 15 knots and a light chop. As we approached Newport's little Castle Hill Lighthouse, another big, bad idea bubbled up into my think tank.

Our pre-trip research had revealed that the LYDIA SCHOLFIELD, a massive square-rigger carrying cotton oil, had wrecked in the late 1800s on Butterball Rock just south of the light. Over the years, scuba divers had described the wreck site, which could also be reached by snorkelers, as a veritable junkyard of nautical debris including ship's nails, hull copper and ship's fittings and hardware. BUCKRAMMER's current position, just abeam of the infamous rock, coupled with the calm, 74-degree seas made a dive stop totally irresistible. I explained the situation to Caroline, who was busily making ham and cheese sandwiches for our lunch in the galley.

Caroline Conway prepares to dive on the LYDIA SCHOFIELD shipwreck off of Newport, RI.

"What say we give this wreck a look-see?"

"Sort of a dry run for Brenton Cove, only wet?" she punned.

"Er, right," I groaned.

Within minutes we were out of the shipping channel and securely anchored behind the old Butterball itself in about 10 to 15 feet of water with two, building cases of wreck fever. We had noticed a current flowing in toward Newport, so we took the precaution of reeling out about 400 feet of buoyant, yellow polypropylene rope with a float ball tied to the bitter end. This line would give us a little extra margin of safety should the current pick up.

After lunch we donned masks, snorkels and fins and took the plunge by following the anchor line down to the seabed. One look around the bottom confirmed the diver's reports. Even after all these years, hundreds of yellowish ship's nails, from little 2-inch tacks to foot-long spikes, had accumulated in the nooks and crannies between the rocks. Every now and then, a piece of ship copper would come into view. Caroline and I spent a pleasant forty-five minutes repeatedly diving off of BUCKRAMMER's bow, descending to the bottom, and riding the current while stuffing the zip-lock bags we carried with artifacts. We would then surface near the end of the poly-rope and pull ourselves back to dump our booty and repeat the process. On one such run, I spied a large, cross-shaped piece with machined holes that was too heavy to lift easily. I noted its location and on a subsequent run I tied the bitter end of a separate 30-foot length of poly-rope through one of the holes and let the free end float to the surface to serve as a marker.

Around 3:00 P.M., exhausted by the diving and chilled by Narragansett Bay, we called it quits and climbed into the cockpit to examine our finds. Caroline, always good with numbers, conducted the analysis.

"Geez Dad, looks like we have about 243 ship's nails of various sizes, 5 foot-long bronze timber spikes, 4 bronze drift pins, a length of standing rigging"—this was steel wire parceled with hemp, burlap and sail cloth, all soaked in pitch-black tar—"and about 5 square feet of copper hull plating. Not a bad haul."

"Don't forget that big boy over there," I said referring to the mysterious object tied to the end of the poly-rope. "Let's see what that is."

We snagged the rope with a boat hook and, by putting our backs into it, landed all twenty-five-plus pounds of the "thing from two fathoms" in short order.

"Whadaya suppose it is?" Caroline asked.

"Beats the tar out of me," I puzzled. "Maybe some nautical historian will be able to tell us when we get back. Meanwhile it makes one heck of a curio." We stowed away our treasures, tidied up a bit, weighed anchor and headed once more toward Newport Harbor, Brenton Cove and *real* treasure.

To this day no one has been able to definitively identify the function of this cast and machined bronze piece. The best guess is that it is the rudder-mounted fitting of the chain "keeper" that prevented the LYDIA SCHOLFIELD's rudder from unseating. (For example, see the cover photo of SULTANA in *WoodenBoat* magazine #165.) Perhaps some sharp reader will provide a better explanation.

Brenton Cove's Cove

Few would deny that Newport, Rhode Island is one of the most amazing yachting centers in the world. Within its well-sheltered, deepwater confines lie every service and amenity imaginable to the visiting boater . . . for a price. Since BUCK-RAMMER operates more or less on a seltzer budget, a harbor such as Newport presents a daunting pecuniary challenge. Fortunately, Bucky's captain had perfected the fine art of mooring mooching. In this case he was able to convince a local friend to loan out his anchorage, right in the target area, for two nights. The price? A mere bottle of good (but not too good) Burgundy. The target area was a little cove in the southernmost corner of Brenton Cove, right across from the old ropewalk at Fort Adams. On our wonderfully situated mooring, we could almost throw a small stone and hit the cliff above the resting place of the "treasure ship."

Not bad! Well, actually, there was a bit of bad news, namely that the mooring was situated a mile or so from the Newport waterfront. Fortunately, we had towed our little, 10-foot pram, SPLINTER, with us to Newport and had the foresight to mount our 4 hp outboard on her transom. So in almost less time than it takes to explain it, Caroline and I changed for dinner, climbed into the little boat and motored over to the dinghy dock at the Ann Street pier. It was an easy fifteen-minute jaunt.

We secured the vessel and within minutes found ourselves facing plates of spaghetti at Sala's Dining Room ("spaghetti-by-the-pound") on Thames Street. Between slurps, we planned the next day's treasure hunt on the back of Sala's paper placemats. An hour or so later, and two pounds of "sketties" heavier, we had our dive mapped out and decided to celebrate with some dessert. Past experience told us that the best desserts would be found by snooping around the piers outside. So we settled up the dinner bill, waddled down the stairs and flowed north into the Thames Street scene.

The Newport waterfront has been lovingly transformed over the past thirty years from a somewhat ramshackle collection of rotting piers and local bars into a Disney-esque village of retail shops, restaurants, marinas and boat-related commercial enterprises. The place really comes alive at night with attractions that range from family fare to more mature offerings.

Caroline and I roamed around, checking out a few of our favorite haunts. I felt a tad embarrassed for my daughter, stuck with the old man and all. Yet she didn't seem to mind. Maybe this bonding thing was working. After a fashion (and a few stops at clothing, army surplus, gift and art stores with Caroline), we somehow ended up in front of a Ben & Jerry's ice cream stand. Caroline and I each got a double scoop, planted ourselves on a dockside bench and engaged in some serious people watching as we pecked at the cones. This treasure hunting business was hard work.

It took a little longer to motor back to BUCKRAMMER, what with the dark and all but within thirty-five minutes of leaving the dinghy dock, Caroline and I were snug under the covers in our bunks, dreaming of tomorrow's treasure hunt. I drifted off thinking that this had been the kind of "messing about" day that makes boating my favorite pastime.

Treasure Day Arrives

As is the tradition on BUCKRAMMER, the morning began with a fisherman's breakfast of bacon, eggs, toast and coffee, all cooked on our dependable, coal-fired Shipmate stove. In the cockpit we revisited the plans made the previous night as we sopped up egg yolks with toast.

"If everything I've been told holds true, then the treasure wreck lies in about 15 feet of water just at the base of that cliff," I said pointing to a spot on the water about 100 feet away from our boat. "We can just leave BUCKRAMMER tied to the mooring and snorkel over from here."

A little put off by my matter-of-fact attitude, Caroline jokingly replied, "Ten-four Commander. I roger that plan—just like I did last night, you big Twinkie"

"OK, OK," I replied wincing. "Let's get our gear on and get wet."

As per "the plan," Caroline and I quickly swam over to the base of the cliff and regrouped on a little ledge-like outcropping at the cliff's base for a last safety check of each other's gear. Even by 9:00 A.M., the waters of Brenton Cove's cove were a comfortable 78 degrees.

"Ready to take the plunge?" I asked.

"All set maestro," Caroline shot back. "Last one to the bottom is a rotten worm shoe." And down she went.

Not to be out-dived (or is it out-doven?) by a mere teenager, I executed a little back flip and swiftly submerged as well. As the sun had not yet peeked over the crest of the cliff, the underwater visibility was limited to about 6 feet. The bottom consisted of a mix of mud and sand, easily disturbed into silty clouds by my swim fins. It took a few seconds for my eyes to adjust to the light and focus, but when they did I was surprised by what I saw. It appeared as though we were surrounded by all manner of old bottles, cups, plates and metal parts. A brigade of spider crabs and a number of perch-like cunner fish stood guard over the whole lot. Both Caroline and I carried nylon mesh laundry bags to hold any "treasures" encountered underwater. With a few seconds of breath remaining, I quickly grabbed several of the bottles and an old cup and saucer, dropped them into the bag and shot to the surface. I repeated this exercise a few dozen times until the mesh bag held about twenty pounds of assorted schtuff. Then I swam back to the ledge to wait for Caroline and to check out the haul.

Caroline swam about 75 feet further north along the cliff. From my perch on the ledge I could see that she was also finding lots of artifacts as she made a series of thirty-second dives. Within ten minutes she swam back to the ledge as well. Caroline flipped her mask up onto her brow.

"Holy cow! I'm not sure whether this is a wreck or an underwater flea market. What gives with this place?"

I had been puzzling the same thing ever since my first plunge. "Beats me!" I replied. "I haven't seen even a hint of the actual shipwreck, just mounds of glassware and other bric-a-brac. If this is a shipwreck, the vessel must have been carrying one strange cargo."

With this we decided to examine our finds. Sure enough, Caroline and I had together bagged a total of about thirty pounds of glass bottles, china and metalware. While most of it was cracked or broken or rusted into amorphous masses, some of the pieces were in good enough condition to be considered collectible. We placed the best pieces on the ledge and returned the rest to the sea.

Caroline pondered the riddle. "Maybe the wreck is further out in the cove and all this stuff is her 'debris field.' Why don't we explore a larger area?"

This sounded reasonable to me. "Tell you what," I said. "Let's put the good junk back into our bags, then do as you suggest and expand our search. If we find more high-quality debris along the way, we'll put it in our bags. If you come across the remains of the wreck, give a holler and I'll do the same. If we don't find the wreck, then head back to BUCK-RAMMER when you get cold. OK?"

"Cool!"

About forty-five minutes later both of us were back in BUCKRAMMER's cockpit giving the sun a chance to work its warming magic. While we had once again filled our respective bags with lots of interesting salvage, neither of us had seen anything that even remotely looked like a shipwreck.

Caroline and I, each wrapped in beach towels and sitting cross-legged on the cockpit floor, rummaged through and sorted our haul. Suddenly, from out of nowhere, a voice rang out.

"Invite me on board and I'll tell you where to find the wreck."

My daughter and I looked at one another, eyes wide, and then simultaneously sprang to our feet.

Cappy Marks the Spot

"Well, are ya gonna ask me aboard or did I row this whole gad-blasted way for diddly-squat-a-nooyears?"

My daughter and I found ourselves eyeball-to-eyeball

with one of the saltiest old codgers seen on any waterfront by us before or since. He bobbed alongside BUCKRAMMER in a leaky old skiff accompanied by a scruffy little dog that looked like twenty miles of bad road. We grabbed the painter of the little boat as this curious character hauled himself over our catboat's gunwales.

"Name's Fred Crowell, Captain Fred Crowell, late of the Shell Oil tugboat service. You can call me Cappy. Who are yer?" We made our introductions.

"Ahab an I wus watch'n yer frum the ol fort over there an figgered you were look'n fer the ol wreck. Well I'll tell yer this. It sure as blazes ain't where you wus swim'n 'round."

Captain Crowell fixed the more controllable of his two eyes on us all squinty-like and smiled a jack-o'-lantern smile. Ahab gave out a little condescending snort from his perch in the skiff.

"But I tell yer wot. Fix me sumpfin to ett and a cup of Joe, hot and black, and I'll put you right on top of the ol girl." All things considered, this seemed like a reasonable offer. Worst case, perhaps a sandwich and a hot coffee would persuade this guy to row back from whence he came.

As Caroline whipped up a batch of "Dad's Special Tuna" on Italian bread (two cans of tuna fish, juice from one half of a lemon, chopped celery, and one tablespoon of oregano flakes, all mixed with lots of mayonnaise) and I put the percolator on, Captain Crowell told us his story. Ahab had decided to take a snooze under the skiff's rear seat.

In a nutshell, Cappy had spent the better part of his eighty-six years in various merchant marine assignments all over the globe. While any one episode of his life would fill a book or two, the one most relevant to our treasure hunt took place during World War II when he was stationed at Fort Adams for a few months during the summer of 1944. For recreation, he and the other swabbies would take a dip in the cove where we were now moored. A few of the gang, Cappy among them, had waterproofed some aviator's goggles and used them to explore the depths. During these dives they had found not one but three wrecks in the cove.

In his spare time, the captain had done some research on the wrecks. He had learned that "our" wreck was a ship purchased long ago by the owner of the cliff-top mansion in a derelict condition but fully ballasted with cobblestones. She was stripped of spars and valuable hardware and then scuttled at the base of the cliff for use as (gads!) *a dock footing*. The pilings are marked on the Brenton Cove map.

Pop went our notions of silver and gold.

Of the two remaining wrecks, Cappy had only been able to positively identify one, the JEM, a slave trader (like the infamous AMISTAD). JEM, set ablaze under suspicious circumstances, sank in the cove sometime before the Civil War. The identity of the third wreck remained an enigma.

Cappy lit up a slightly smushed stogie and, using the burned-out match as a pointer, directed our attention to the base of the cliff.

"You was swimm'n on the garbage dump of the ol mansion. See, they used to jest throw their trash right off-en that cliff into what they must have figger'd wus the bottomless sea. All of that junk you've got here in yer cockpit is jest household rubbish of rich people from the olden days." Cappy shifted his pointing to a spot about 400 feet to the right and south, toward a dock at the base of another part of the same cliff.

"If you want to be poking around the ol wreck, then you want to be swimm'n right over there. See those dock pilings?" Caroline and I nodded.

"Those pilings go straight through the center hold of the ol girl. You can't miss her even if'n you tried."

Mouths somewhat agape, my daughter and I thought about this for a few seconds and then said, "Let's go diving!"

Cappy, grabbing an extra sandwich, offered to row us over. Soon we found ourselves on the dock float supposedly right above the wreck. Caroline was first to don her diving gear and enter the water. In a few seconds she surfaced wearing an ear-to-ear smile.

"Captain Crowell, you are dead on! Dad, we've got one of the prettiest little schooner wrecks right under your feet. What are you waiting for?"

I squinched my flippers on and dove in. Sure enough! Directly beneath the dock we found an amazingly well pre-served wreck of a clipper-bowed schooner of about 95 feet skewered by the pilings. She had sunk into the mud such that her decks were flush with the bottom of the cove. My daughter and I spent the better part of an hour probing the lost ship. Though we didn't find any "specie," in the process of examining the old girl we became familiar enough with her layout to draw mental pictures of what she must have looked like in her prime. She had been a beauty. Though it seemed a shame that this forgotten little vessel would serve out her final days as the foundation of a dock, at least she had not been lost forever in some shipbreaker's yard. In-stead, she still plied the waters, pointing south and outward bound.

Cappy rowed Caroline and me back to BUCKRAMMER. On the way he told us how to find both the wreck of the JEM and the third, unknown wreck (which he estimated might be as old as the Revolutionary War based on some of the arti-facts that he and his sailor friends had salvaged back in the 1940s). But cold and tired, Caroline and I would leave these explorations for another day. Thanks to the kindness of this ancient mariner, Caroline and I had discovered most of what we had sought ('cept the silver and gold, of course).

Captain Crowell and Ahab dropped us off on BUCKRAM-MER and bid us safe passage. I offered to buy him dinner, but he said that he had big plans for that evening. He would take another cup of coffee, however, black and hot. Some months later we learned that Cappy had passed away among friends in his home in Providence, Rhode Island about three weeks after our adventure. As of 2001, Ahab was still among the living, instructing Cappy's grandnephews in the fine art of dog nurturing.

That evening BUCKRAMMER's captain and crew got dressed in our Sunday best, rowed to the innermost end of the cove and beached SPLINTER. We then trudged up the road to the elegant Castle Hill Inn and Resort (www.castlehillinn.com), where we enjoyed a Gatsby-style, multicourse meal. Over dessert, sumptuous strawberry shortcake, we reluctantly planned our return to Westport on the morning tide.

After supper, Caroline and I sat on the grassy knoll outside the restaurant and looked across Rhode Island Sound toward Block Island as the sun capped off a remarkable day with a spectacular sunset.

"Well Dad, this has been quite a weekend. I'm afraid, however, that you'll still have to work your day job. No doubloons or pieces of eight. No treasure on this trip."

Looking Caroline in the face, I gave her a little, misty-eyed wink and a hug.

"Oh, I wouldn't be so sure about that. I wouldn't be so sure."

6

—◦✸◦—

Return of the Coggeshalls

"Ah! Just the man I'm looking for."

Captain Cal Perkins dashed across the exhibit hall at the annual meeting of the Catboat Association. He thrust a beat-up, postcard-sized envelope into my hand. With a smile as broad as Block Island Sound, Cal said, "You are not going to believe who sent this and what they want to do." A bit befuddled by Cal's charge, I opened the envelope, withdrew the letter within and began to read.

Dear Mr. Perkins:

Last summer a friend of mine lent me his copy of "The Family, Me and the Cat," John Conway's article about the catboat that he had bought from you. Upon reading the story, I was thrilled to realize that this was the same boat my father owned from March 1937 to September 1952. The pictures in the article made me feel like a boy again instead of seventy!

The history of the boat, as outlined in the piece, was of great interest to me. Sadly, most of my father's records of the earlier and later history of BUCKRAMMER *disappeared from his files when he retired. So, much of this information that Mr. Conway revealed was new to me. However, I still do have some of the records from those years when he owned the boat. Please allow me to share some of their content with you.*

My father bought BUCKRAMMER *as the* JOSEPHINE S *from Lester Watson in March of 1937. In June of that year, Lester's son, a student at Harvard, and three of his classmates and friends sailed the boat from Marion to Barnstable. My dad, my brother Wells and I met them at the Sandwich boat basin (eastern end of the Cape Cod Canal) and on the final leg of the journey, they showed us the ropes. I already had a Beetle Cat of my own, but this was a real yacht!*

That next weekend, sitting around at the dinner table, we decided to rechristen our new boat PELICAN. *It was my mother's suggestion. She noted that the boat's cockpit was larger than the cabin and she recited the old rhyme, "A remarkable bird is the pelican, whose beak can hold more than its belly-can." (As an aside, we surely would have renamed the boat* ESTHER *had we known, as I now know, that this was* BUCK-RAMMER'S *original name. You see, Mr. Perkins, my mother's name was Esther! How about that?!)*

During the next fifteen years, my two brothers, Wells and Clarke, my sister Carol and I had many wonderful cruises on the PELICAN. *After the '38 hurricane, my father had the boat rebuilt by the Kelly Boatyard in Fairhaven. The cost to the insurance company was $2,000, a handsome sum in those days. Seven years later, the Crosby yard did a major refit, installing a new Kermatt engine.*

My dad dearly loved that boat of his, but he was not a particularly competent sailor. Family lore remembers him as usually landing on a rock or shoal whenever he set sail without a son to guide him. Per-

haps this is why, in 1952, with his children grown up and involved with their own lives, he found PELICAN *too often idle on her mooring and in an impulsive moment sold her.*

The new owner was a Mr. Henry Hope of Bloomington, Indiana, an art historian. He's the one who had the pelican figurehead carved by a student of his, Hal Carney of New Orleans.

My father used the proceeds of the sale to subsidize cruising charters in the 1950s along the coast of eastern Maine. Each summer, my brothers and I would join our dad for a wonderful cruise, providing him with a competent skipper and crew. He called himself "The Swabbie."

Over the decades that followed, in all of my journeys along the coast in my own boats, I only saw PELICAN *twice. Her lines and bowsprit and porthole configuration were (and still are) unmistakable. Once was at the Niantic marina in Essex, Connecticut in the late '60s. The other time was in Vineyard Haven, as I recall. No one was on board either time to see the joy that I felt at viewing this marvelous token from my boyhood.*

Before he sold PELICAN, *my father commissioned John Howard, Jr. to fashion a model of the old catboat. That model hangs to this day on the wall behind my favorite chair. She was truly my first love!*

I found your mailing address from the Catboat Association but have not been able to locate Mr. Conway's. If you would be kind enough to forward his address, I'd love to make contact with him . . . and maybe arrange to see our boat in her latest reincarnation.

Sincerely,
Tim Coggeshall

As I read the letter Cal looked over my shoulder and reread it himself.

Upon finishing, we both looked up and simultaneously muttered. 'Wow!"

Crosby's Cedar Time Machine

"No way! You're pulling my leg, right?"

I returned from the annual meeting and showed my better half, Chris, the letter. She could hardly believe that, through some celestial alignment, BUCKRAMMER's former owners had rediscovered the old bucket and her new caretakers—us!

My heart raced. "I've got to contact these people."

A call to "411" supplied Tim Coggeshall's phone number and I dialed away. Repeated calls went unanswered, and no answering machine kicked in for me to leave a message. Frustrated, I drafted a letter of my own, attached it to a large file of photocopied ESTHER-JOSEPHINE S-PELICAN-CAPE GIRL-BUCKRAMMER documents that had been collected and assembled by the old girl's former owners and mailed the whole package to Tim's Cape Cod address.

A month passed without a response. Then, toward the end of April, the mail finally brought a reply. The letter had been produced on something akin to a manual Underwood typewriter in need of a good cleaning. I was obviously dealing with a bona fide New England Yankee.

Dear John:

I was delighted to receive your letter and the dossier of materials and information about ESTHER-JOSEPHINE S-PELICAN-CAPE GIRL-BUCKRAMMER and her distinguished history. My wife Luby and I have just returned from a six-week holiday. It took me three days to sort through

*the mountain of accumulated mail, where I finally
came across your letter and folder of documents.*

*My brother Clarke and my sister Carol are both
excited as I am that we will have an opportunity to
reacquaint ourselves with the ancient catboat that we
so dearly loved when youngsters. I am also sure that
among the three of us we will, eventually, locate materials for your historical BUCKRAMMER collection. I
note from your chronology of ownership that the
Coggeshall family had the longest tenure except for
Captain Eldridge (the original owner) himself . . .
who only beat us out by one year!*

*As I write, I am looking at a photo, taken in 1938,
of Luby at PELICAN's wheel, me perched on the coaming beside her—my two early loves, the PELICAN and
the girl that I married six years later. In my boyhood
years, I kept a journal. As a result, I have written accounts of our taking possession of the boat at Sandwich, accounts of our first cruises to Marion, Duxbury
and Provincetown, and of the 1938 hurricane. I also
have a description of my "graduation present" from
Exeter in 1940, a monthlong cruise to Maine with my
two best friends. I will make photocopies of all of these
for you.*

*During World War II, the PELICAN was confined to
Barnstable Harbor. Not long after I returned from
war service in the Pacific, my father, Clarke, Luby
and I cruised to Annisquam on her. This was Luby's
first real cruise. It was a miracle that she continued to
sail with me for the next fifty years, because the errant
boom almost swept her overboard as we were franti-
cally trying to lash the gigantic sail in a fierce thun-
der-squall off Plymouth. Clarke will be able to tell you
about his cruise to Maine with two Harvard buddies
in 1952 not long before my father suddenly sold the
boat to Henry Hope. Our fifteen years of "custodian-*

ship" (your word in the article) created many memo-
ries. I must say, we thought of the boat as being "old"
fifty years ago.

In one of my father's letters in your collection (a
letter that I had never seen before), he concludes his
remarks to the new owner of PELICAN, *in the context of*
the expense of maintaining a wooden boat: "I prefer
boats to golf or blondes as a favorite vice." I guess he
did, for both he and my mother continued to cruise
with me on my own boat, DAUNTLESS, *until they were*
almost eighty, once to Cape Breton. My mother re-
membered her father and his four brothers sailing to
Newfoundland from Boston in the 1870s on their
English-style cutter, KITTEN. *Now that was real adven-*
turing!

Obviously, my family would love to visit our old
cedar friend. My sister lives right next door. Clarke
lives outside of Boston but is a summertime resident
with his wife, Eddie, in the barn on our property. Un-
doubtedly we can make ourselves available some time
during the summer when we are all together, at your
convenience of course.

Clarke, Carol and I look forward to meeting you.
That roomy cockpit could also probably accommo-
date Luby and Eddie too, don't you think?

In the meanwhile, we will assemble material for
your BUCKRAMMER *archives.*

Best Wishes,
Tim

I read the letter several times, savoring Tim Coggeshall's
PELICAN-BUCKRAMMER anecdotes more and more with each
reread. Within a few days, we sent back a letter inviting Tim,
Wells, Carol and anyone else in the extended Coggeshall
clan to make the pilgrimage to Westport. Shortly before the

date selected for the visit, I received another letter that supplied additional lore for the BUCKRAMMER archives.

Dear John:

In advance of our trip to Westport I wanted to share a recent anecdote that you may find hard to believe. A few weeks ago, at a social function, I was seated at a table with another elderly gentleman, a stranger to me. In our subsequent conversation we stumbled on our shared love of sailing. I told him I'd owned a Beetle Cat since 1932. He mentioned that he had learned to sail on his family's catboat in the early 1930s on Buzzard's Bay. I told him that I had the same experience on Cape Cod Bay, starting in 1937. Soon we discovered that we were talking about the same boat—his family's JOSEPHINE S, our family's PELICAN (your BUCKRAMMER). My table companion was a Watson. In 1937 he was a college student. I was a high school freshman. On June 6, 1937, he and three family friends turned over the JOSEPHINE S to my dad, my brother and me at the Sandwich Boat Basin as I reported in my previous letter to you. They had indeed sailed from Marion, and they were the ones who had stayed on board for the twelve miles to Barnstable Harbor, helping make us familiar with the boat and her gear. Now, sixty years later, we were reminiscing about that distant day when we were young. Truly amazing!

Anyway, the Coggeshalls are looking forward to greeting PELICAN's current owner. We don't require a sail but we'd like to pat the old girl, reminisce a bit and take a few photos. I will bring along my PELICAN file and some excerpts of her log.

Best Wishes,
Tim

Days of Yesteryear Redux

After much too long a waiting period, C day finally arrived,
a magnificent, New England fall masterpiece with a Kodak
sky, 10 to 15 knot winds and temperatures in the low 70s.
The tides had also cooperated in that an incoming, afternoon
flood would allow me to pull BUCKRAMMER up into Slaight's
inlet and the dock there. This would facilitate the Coggeshall
gang's boarding, inspection and sail. Captain Gene Kennedy
had volunteered to act as "swabbie," as Tim's late father
would have put it. And a "foine" swabbie he was too.

A few minutes after noon, the Coggeshall car pulled into
Slaight's driveway and, slowly, Tim, Luby, Wells and Carol
got out and made their way down the grassy slope to the
pier. I was still oiling the interior cabin sole with pine tar
when Captain Gene bellowed from BUCKRAMMER's cockpit,
"Hey Conway! Methinks you've got company."

I bolted out through the doghouse, hopped onto the
dock and ran up the gangplank. Midway up the slope, I
doffed my gritty Red Sox cap and extended my pitch-cov-
ered hand to the descending group.

Tim Coggeshall, a trim, well-tanned specimen of Cape
Cod Yankee, his eyes full of tears, thrust out his hand as well.

"Captain Conway, I presume?"

I could only manage a teary-eyed "Yes sir!" We shook
hands for what seemed a lifetime, our eyes locked. Then
Captain Tim Coggeshall introduced the rest of the family to
Gene and me.

"So there's the old girl, eh?" Tim finally whispered.
"Gawd, she looks just like she did in 1952. Let's get closer,
shall we?"

The whole entourage literally bounded—not bad for a
group of seventy-somethings—down the gangplank and
onto BUCKRAMMER. For over an hour they poked and prodded, peeked and pecked, all the while regaling Gene and
me with one great story after another. In the process we

learned that our bosun's locker had once been a water cistern and that the door to the head was only a curtain while BUCKRAMMER was PELICAN. That the coal stove had been rotated 90 degrees since the olden days. That the cleat near the mainsheet was as much a mystery to the Coggeshalls as it was to us, and so on and so forth. Overall, the Coggeshalls pronounced that the current state of the boat exceeded their wildest expectations as to fit and finish. Wells reiterated that they all had figured that the boat had been lost in one of the hurricanes over the past few decades. "Not bad for a wreck, if I do say so," he piped in.

Gene broke the first wave of reverie with a bellow, "Let's stop the jaw'n and get a sail'n or we'll never get back to the dock on time." As usual Captain Kennedy was spot on. The fair tide allowed only a narrow window if we wanted to take a cruise and return to Slaight's without running aground.

Without a moment's hesitation, the Coggeshalls took their favorite positions (Tim at the helm, Luby to his left, Wells to his right and Carol on the bowsprit), and we started the diesel and headed out into the Westport River and Rhode Island Sound. Just outside the entrance to Westport Harbor, Gene and I hoisted and trimmed sail, doused the engine and handed control over to the Clan.

Over the next few hours, Tim, Luby, Wells and Carol, each in turn, took a trick at the wheel. As Gene and I watched, decades melted away and the Coggeshalls morphed into teens once more. During one tack, Tim gave me a little wink and cautioned, "Watch this."

Quick as a cat, he gave the helm a little wiggle and sent a wall of green water splashing up over the bowsprit and sister Carol perched there. I winced but Carol merely turned around with a huge smile from ear to ear. Tim winked again. "She always loved me to do that."

And so it went.

For a delightful few hours, the Coggeshalls tacked, jibed, heeled and hauled the great, old woodpile just as

The Coggeshall family returns to the cockpit of "Pelican" . . . 50 years after their last visit. (L/R) Luby Coggeshall, Captain Gene Kennedy, Jr., Wells Coggeshall, Tim Coggeshall and Carol Coggeshall.

they had back in the late 1930s, scampering over every inch of the vessel. Luby observed, "It's like we never left the old PELICAN."

Once again it was Gene who injected reality. "Sorry everyone, but you know the old saying about time and tide. If we don't get Bucky back into Slaight's you may have to spend the night."

For an instant, the wonderful thought of a PELICAN sleepover flashed through the imaginations of four blue-haired sailors. But, unfortunately, maturity won out, the boat's helm was put over, and we headed home.

A Parting Gift

Once safely back at Slaight's dock, Tim pulled a large folder out of his duffle bag. "This contains copies of everything that I could find about our old PELICAN. Let's have a look, shall we?"

For almost an hour, Tim and his family showed us copies of old photographs, logbooks and other memorabilia of those

long-ago days when BUCKRAMMER was PELICAN and summers
for the Coggeshalls meant catboating out of Barnstable Harbor, Cape Cod. Of these materials, some of the most remarkable were the journal entries made by Tim during the '30s.

At that time, Tim was in the practice of keeping a hand-
written diary of his day-to-day adventures. Miraculously,
these journals survive. In the weeks leading up to his visit,
Tim had been patient and kind enough to scan through a
decade's worth of entries to find and copy those that per-
tained to PELICAN. As our afternoon with the Coggeshalls
wound down, there in the very cockpit where he and his
siblings (and future bride) actually experienced the adventures, Tim closed out the day by reading a few of these from
the "glory years" of 1937–38:

March 5, 1937: Bought PELICAN
Father has bought a swell catboat, and man o man is she
a beauty! Engine, cabin, stove, ice box, etc. Gee, what
fun we shall have.

June 6, 1937: Boat to Barnstable
After dinner the entire family drove over to the Cape Cod
Canal through which our boat was coming. We went in
order to see if we could get on the boat and sail the rest
of the way to Barnstable. We succeeded and Father,
Uncle Karl, Wells and I got on board and went the rest
of the way with the four boys who were sailing her over.
Boy is this boat swell!

June 13, 1937: First Sail
Father arrived from New York early this morning. He can
only spend one day here today. We all went on a trip in
the new boat. We sailed about 15 miles outside the harbor. Boy, it was neat fun! We brought along our lunch
and made a regular picnic out of it. It was our first real
trip on the PELICAN.

July 7, 1937: First Cruise

Got up early this morning and had breakfast on the boat. Father came aboard early and we weighed anchor for Provincetown. There wasn't much breeze so we used the motor most of the way. Boy, it was neat fun! We arrived in Provincetown Harbor at noon . . . actually a little bit later. After a swim, eating lunch and loading up with gasoline, we hoisted sail for home. Sailed partway and used the motor partway. We had supper on the way and arrived in Barnstable Harbor a little after eight o'clock. Everyone had a wonderful time.

July 22, 1938: Following Year's P-Town Adventure

Father roused us out early this morning with the news that we were going to sail PELICAN to Provincetown. That sounded swell so we got all of the food collected and Bill, Father, Wells and I set sail into a spanking breeze that blew right behind us all of the way. We made Provincetown in good time, but not without encountering some nasty weather. The waves were huge. They just picked us up and slapped us down. [Once in the harbor] we threw our anchor over after filling up our water tank. After furling the sail and getting everything onboard shipshape, Father cooked a neat meal of hamburger, beans and soup. Wells, who had been seasick on the way over, recovered sufficiently to eat also. Bill and Wells and I got "shore leave" and we toured the town "à pied." We also looked for Hugh, who was supposed to have arrived to get on board and sail home with us tomorrow. No luck!

July 23, 1938: The Adventure Continues

Father again roused us out early this morning. Oh yes! Hugh came aboard late last evening. He, by luck, found a man who knew where our boat was and used that man's tender to come out to PELICAN. Now, after eating a neat breakfast cooked by Father, we hoisted the sail (one reef) and headed for home. Outside of Provincetown Harbor we found a terrific wind and huge waves. Pretty soon our tender was swamped. We tried towing the sunken tender behind us but finally were forced to cut her adrift in order to make any headway at all. Almost all of us felt pretty lousy, but no one lost lunch. Hugh was the only one who dared to eat anything all day. The waves were so big that we hardly made any headway and by evening we were still quite a way from home. We put into a small harbor at Dennis, and I called up Mom to come and get us. We couldn't possibly have made Barnstable before it got dark. What a cruise!

September 2, 1938: First Solo Cruise
Took the PELICAN out myself today (by motor). I went outside the point to the red bell buoy. Then a fog came in and I lost the point from sight. Gad! I couldn't find the compass and I didn't know which way I was heading. I just kept going until I found a fish net. Knowing that the long line of net stretches almost into shoal, I followed the poles in. Finally the shoal loomed up before me, but still I didn't have the slightest idea where I was. I cruised along the shoal a way and finally saw a couple of people walking along. I hollered over to them, and they said that I was just off Dennis going in the wrong direction from Barnstable. I had just gone about 8 miles from where I thought I was heading! Well, I followed the shore back to the harbor and from then on it was easy. I was pretty scared for a while, though.

September 26, 1938: The '38 Hurricane
Mom wrote me today. The PELICAN luckily was not lost in the hurricane last week. The boathouse it was stored in floated away, but the PELICAN floated away with it and was finally secured.

Tim closed the folder, cleared his throat and declared, "OK everyone. Time to get back to the twenty-first century."

Gene Kennedy and I accompanied the family up the bank and back to their car. We invited the Coggeshalls to make this *at least* an annual ritual, and they promised that they would. Saying our goodbyes, we watched them head back up the road, back toward the Cape and back into the twenty-first century. That was almost five years ago. BUCK-RAMMER and we still await their return.

7

———〜〜〜———

Squeaking by in
Buzzard's Bay

"Here, take this copy and don't tell anyone where you got it." Tim Lund thrust a folded, rumpled, multipage photocopy into my hand. When I began to unfold it, Tim's hand quickly snapped the document closed.

"You goofball! Put that away until you get home. What are you trying to do, get me in trouble with the Association, or worse, my Dad?" I stuck the thing into my empty canvas bag. "OK, OK! Take it easy!"

The origins of many BUCKRAMMER adventures can be traced to the annual February Catboat Convention, where I presently found myself. This year would prove no different.

At home the following day, I culled the mysterious Lund manuscript from a bag now full of catalogs, brochures and other detritus picked up during the meeting. A quick examination revealed that I held a ten-chapter treatise on the best places to gunkhole a catboat in Buzzard's Bay. An accompanying note from Tim explained that its author, Captain Jeremy B. Whitney, had submitted the article to the editorial board of the Catboat Association's quarterly magazine for publication. Following the advice of a few lawyer-members, the Association had decided not to publish the work due to the challenging nature of its recommendations. Tim explained, "Boats and people *could* get hurt attempting to visit these secret locations. That's why I immediately thought of you and BUCKRAMMER. These are places to *die* for!"

Hmmm. I dug out my nautical charts and examined each of the spots recommended by the manuscript:

- Lackey's Bay: A Tarpaulin Cove for shoal–draft boats but surrounded by rocks.
- Pasque Island Marsh: An exquisitely beautiful spot with a torturous approach.
- Merill's Harbor: The ultimate private place with fabulous but dangerous scenery.
- Penikese Island: A former leper colony but the most underrated harbor in the bay.
- West End Pond: A pudding stone-lined historical oasis.
- Allen's Pond: The best sluice ride in New England, just a bugger to get into.
- Slocum River: A shrine for great horned owls guarded by an extensive bar.
- West Island: Half-settled, half-wild, an outstanding overnight stop.
- Northwest Gutter: A sublime anchorage protected by Rattlesnake Point.

The Association had been right. These gunkholes were among the most dangerous places to operate a small boat. Strong currents, unforgiving rock piles, hull-grabbing sandbars, and keel-kicking ledges infested every location. But, the author swore that he had personally explored each and every spot and had devised a way in and out of them all. His delightful manuscript even included maps and ranges. If he were actually telling the truth, these places offered anyone willing to put his skills to the test some of the most secluded and picturesque cruising on the eastern seaboard. We *had* to give them a shot.

Into the Danger Zone

Throughout the remainder of the spring, my family and I planned our assault on Jeremy's Holes, as we had come to know them. Each had its own window of opportunity. Some could only be attempted with several days of guaranteed offshore winds. (In Buzzard's Bay? Yeah, right.) Others required an astronomically high spring tide as the admission ticket. Even the "easy" ones demanded skillful navigation based on informal and indistinct references such as trees and boulders. (For instance: "when, from your boat's eye view, the scrub oak aligns with the large rock on the beach in front of the oak, your vessel will lie in the channel. If you hold this heading until your boat passes the pine tree on the point of land to the right, then you will avoid collision with the reef submerged from view in the pseudo-channel.")

We carefully laid out the parameters of each prospective assault. On the full moon tide, we would try Allen's Pond. When the wind blew strongly from the southeast, the Northwest Gutter would be worth a try. And so on.

Great weather, in conjunction with a late May spring tide, provided the first open window, and we jumped through it with fearful spunk: BUCKRAMMER would explore (drum roll, please) . . . the Slocum River. The river lies at the northwestern end of Slocum's Bay, a natural formation adjacent to our own Westport in the coastal town of South Dartmouth.

It took less than two hours to sail a fully loaded BUCKRAMMER from our mooring at Westport Point to Potomska Point, a spit of land that acts as a sentry to the Slocum's River Preserve. We chose this area as our first site mostly due to what Captain Whitney characterized as "the shrine-like nature of the place to catboaters." As Whitney pointed out in his gunkhole guide, it was from here, in 1912, that Henry Plummer, his son and their cat had set sail for Florida aboard the MASCOT, an adventure chronicled in the historic book *The Boy, Me and the Cat*. We also hoped that the sheltered, sandy-bottomed river would be a forgiving place to practice before the more challenging locations.

Whitney described two approaches in his guide, one accessible from the north side of the point, the other directly across a barrier bar and only open during high tide. We decided to cross the bar. Caroline took a position on the bowsprit to look out for rocks or other obstructions (the chart showed a few, randomly placed, submerged pilings). The rest of the gang, my wife Chris, my daughter Abby and my son Ned, kept an eye on the port, the starboard and the depth-sounder, respectively. To give ourselves a little wiggle room, we decided to make the bar-crossing attempt about an hour before high tide. This way, if we did run aground, Mother Nature would slide a little extra water under our keel to help us become unstuck. Ned continuously called out the depth in feet. BUCKRAMMER needed 2 proud feet to make her way through.

"Six, five, six, four, five, four, six, five." Ned called out. "Six, six, seven, ten, twelve—Dad, I think we're in."

Just as Captain Whitney had predicted, we found ourselves in 10 to 12 feet of clean river with several miles of deep water ahead of us. How about that!

BUCKRAMMER and her crew spent a wonderful day exploring the nooks and crannies of the Slocum's River complex. Again as advertised, we spotted a number of great horned owls snoozing in several grand oaks that dotted the river's edge. That night we anchored near Peleg's Island, about a mile from Potomska Point, and broke out the charcoal grill. During a late supper, we were treated to a spectacularly full "Planter's Moon" rising over the saltmarsh. Captain Whitney had us hooked.

As the summer progressed, the Conway horde conquered one gunkhole after another, with Penikese, Lackey's Bay, Pasque Island Marsh and most of the others succumbing to a combination of expert navigation, daring helmsmanship, plucky perspicacity and plain dumb luck. By late

August every single one of Jeremy's Holes had been conquered but for the evasive and somewhat frightening West
End Pond.

The Best of the Worst Saved for Last

On the tail end of the Elizabeth Island chain lies the isolated
and spectacularly beautiful island of Cuttyhunk. On any
given summer weekend this 5-square-mile chunk of real es-
tate draws literally hundreds of boaters and thousands of visitors to her charming beaches and harbors.

Most mariners who stop at this enchanted place spend
the night in the inner or outer parts of the main harbor on
the northern end of the island. Few are aware of a third, sea-
connected harbor on Cuttyhunk's south shore, shown on the
charts as West End Pond.

Situated on the southern section of the island, the pond
once served as a moat for a fortress built in 1602 on what is
now Gosnold Island. Explorer Bartholomew Gosnold and
his English colonists erected the rampart to protect themselves from potentially hostile Native Americans. Today, an
impressive stone monument on the island serves as a re-
minder of this long-ago time.

In his manuscript Jeremy Whitney describes West End
Pond as a gunkhole clearly not for everybody. "We are at the
margin here," he says about the advisability of entering this
harbor, but it is the kind of place that "you often think about
just before you lapse into sleep on a cold February night."
The incredible beauty of the place, he says, coupled with the
elation of successfully overcoming the risks of the enterprise,
make West End Pond the Mount Everest of Buzzard's Bay.

We would only get one shot at West End Pond that year.
This occurred during August's spring tide weekend, when as
much as 4 or 5 extra feet of water would raise the low tide
water level (which was bone-dry in the case of West End

Pond). Wind and sea conditions had to be perfect as well. The prevailing south-by-southwest winds generated breakers over the Pond's entrance bar all summer long, providing a superb natural deterrent to all but the surfing crowd. So only an easterly breeze would do, and this occurred only three or four days a month at this time of year. Finally, and perhaps most importantly, BUCKRAMMER needed as many hands as possible to help with navigation, depth-sounding and, if we ran aground, unsticking.

"Don't count on me," Chris warned. "I think you're nuts to even think about pulling a stunt like this. But I know that you have your heart set on The Quest, so just promise that you won't let anyone get hurt when I'm not there, which I will absolutely not be."

"OK!" I promised. "Anyway, the odds are a hundred to one that the planets will align enough for us to give it a go. But, if they do, I'll take care."

Miraculously, align they did, and on a calm, sunny August Saturday, BUCKRAMMER and the Conway crew, minus one mom, cautiously approached the entrance to West End Pond on a bearing toward Eagle Rock, just as dictated by Captain Whitney.

In anticipation of this moment, and with the promise of "safety first" in mind, our catboat had been fitted to the gills with a broad assortment of equipment that a season's worth of gunkholing had revealed as essential. This included:

- Scouting dinghy: our tender the SPLINTER.
- Kedge anchor: the boat's storm anchor with 500 feet of ½-inch nylon and a float.
- Marine lever: a 10-foot 2 by 4 timber for prying boats over sandbars.
- "Breadcrumbs": a few dozen 10-foot lengths of ½-inch PVC plumbing pipe.
- Shallow-draft propulsion: the tender's 4 hp outboard motor.

- Beach shoes: goofy-looking, slipper-like footwear for wading in unknown waters.
- Snorkeling gear: masks, fins and snorkels for underwater engineering work.
- Plus the usual assortment of depth sounder, radios, and so on.

Like some Victorian Age expedition, BUCKRAMMER's assault on West End Pond would proceed in a series of carefully choreographed stages, each supported by our odd collection of tools and implements.

Stage One began with a reconnoitering of the entrance guzzles. We anchored our boat off the inlet about two hours after low tide. With the tide still essentially out, Abby, Ned and I rowed ashore with a boatload of PVC pipe. Caroline stayed with the boat and acted as our lookout.

The shallow water allowed us to wade the entire length of the channel right up to the point where it entered the body of the pond and dropped off to a depth in excess of a fathom (6 feet). Wading up the inlet with the SPLINTER in tow, Abby and I selected pieces of PVC pipe and, at 10-foot intervals, stuck them vertically into the river bottom next to the areas with the deepest water. Ned would then measure about 2 feet up the pole and mark this height with a piece of blue masking tape. We had devised this trick earlier in the season while entering the Northwest Gutter between Uncatena and Naushon Islands. As the tide filled the inlet, the poles would act as channel markers: When the water level had exceeded the blue tape markers, the channel would be BUCKRAMMER-navigable. Abby had coined the term "breadcrumbing" for this technique as, from a distance, the white poles looked all the world like something from Hansel and Gretel. After placing all of our marker poles, we returned to the boat and executed Stage Two.

The second stage involved setting our Northhill storm anchor line and float about 200 feet outside of the inlet's mouth. Once again SPLINTER was called into play. Ned rowed us to a spot near the guzzle's mouth and I lowered and set the anchor; as Ned rowed us back to our catboat, I paid out the line. Once back on board, I tied a small vinyl boat fender to the bitter end of the rope. On the fender we had written with indelible marker, "BUCKRAMMER Kedge Line. Do Not Remove." Here again, a previous gunkholing expedition (to Allen's Pond) had shown us (almost the hard way) the prudence of rigging a way to control how fast the boat entered an inlet. The line would also provide us with a convenient way of pulling our boat out of the inlet on the way back out. It had worked beautifully before and we expected the same at West End Pond.

Stage Three involved digging our 4 hp outboard motor and its bracket out of their locker and securing the motor to BUCKRAMMER's stern. Earlier in the summer, while crossing mudflats in Pasque Island Marsh, we almost blew up Red, Jr. when mud and silt entered the seawater intake and stopped the diesel's cooling system cold. From that day on, we decided to use our little "kicker" as a shallow-water auxiliary. Our lightweight, short-shaft outboard seemed to have been made for mucking through thin water, and it pushed BUCKRAMMER with amazing grace for such a pip-squeak of a thing.

"I love work," Caroline piped up. "I could watch people laboring all day long. But I guess we're done, right?" While protecting BUCKRAMMER from sneak pirate attacks, my youngest daughter had observed the rest of us executing Stages One, Two and Three.

"Yup!" I replied. "Nothing left to do now but wait for the tide to come in. Then the fun can begin in earnest."

We did not have long to wait. Within an hour or so, a jillion gallons of Buzzard's Bay flowed into the West End Pond, raising the water level well beyond the blue tape markers on the poles.

"Hey old man," Abby called out. "What are we waiting for? Fire up the tooter and let's get this bucket underway."

I shot back an "Aye, aye," pulled the ripcord on the outboard and yelled, "Everyone assume your positions."

Ned raced to the bowsprit and pulled in our main anchor. As soon as it had broken free of the bottom, I shifted the engine into gear and swung BUCKRAMMER into position heading directly into the channel. Caroline then changed places with Ned and took over as "bow girl." From this position she had a vantage point that gave her great visibility of the bottom directly ahead of our boat. Ned assumed a position amidships and monitored our left-to-right position in the channel. Abby took hold of the kedge-anchor line and would serve as "brake lady." Finally, I centered BUCKRAMMER's massive rudder then manned the outboard. In this situation, the little motor would both propel and steer the boat. BUCKRAMMER slowly crept into the entrance to West End Pond.

At this point in the tale, the Hyperbole John part of me is tempted to embellish our trip through the guzzle by writing, "near disaster struck almost immediately." Truth is, everything worked beautifully. Over a riverbed that had been almost bone-dry just a few hours earlier, our family-infected woodpile floated like a leaf in a millpond. In less than five minutes, BUCKRAMMER entered the legendary West End Pond and the Conway clan joined the "Bart Gosnold" club. Praise be Captain Whitney.

Florida Comes to New England

West End Pond lived up to its reputation and then some. As directed by the charts in the captain's manuscript, we decided to anchor BUCKRAMMER, bow and stern, behind the south side of Gosnold Island in about 10 feet of 81-degree, crystal-clear water. After a lunch of grilled hot dogs, chips and root beer, the various members of our expedition went about their individual or collective adventures.

Ned rowed over and inspected a vast expanse of oyster lines running to the north end of the pond (part of an attempt to reseed the area, we are told). Abby and Caroline swam to Gosnold Island and surveyed the rubble-stone monument there. Abby was especially keen to see if anything remained of Gosnold's old fortress (sad to say, nothing does). I stayed on the boat and decided to put everything in order for our overnight stay. While tilting the outboard to lift it from the water, I chanced to look down at Red, Jr.'s propeller. Much to my surprise, I saw a small cloud of tropically colored fish picking at something or other growing on the shaft strut. This had to be checked out.

I slipped on a set of swim fins and a mask with snorkel and jumped over the side.

The scene slowly came into focus and revealed a tropical paradise. I counted at least five varieties of fish native to the British Virgin Islands but hardly hardy enough for this part of the world. These included sergeant majors, neon go-

The Conway kids look for Indian artifacts on Gosnold Island on Cuttyhunk.

(L/R) Ned and Abby Conway search Gosnold Pond for wayward tropical fish.

bies, yellow wrasses, French grunts and some black damselfish. When the kids returned from their adventures, I shared what I had discovered, and we all went back into the water for a look. All we can figure is that these fish must have somehow ridden the Gulf Stream north during the early part of the summer, strayed into the pond and set up shop in the warm water. We all shuddered to think what would become of these creatures when winter rolled around.

Dinner consisted of a steak on the grill served with a mixed salad, boiled red potatoes (with scallions) and corn on the cob. A grand strawberry shortcake dessert topped the meal off with a flourish. After dinner, as we lazed about on BUCKRAMMER's deck and cabintop, the full moon rose behind the monument in an impressive imitation of the monolith scene from Stanley Kubrick's classic film *2001: A Space Odyssey*. Not such a bad way to end a pretty full day.

The next morning, on the high tide, we weighed anchor and reversed the process to extract ourselves from the pond. As we passed each breadcrumb marker pole, Ned pulled it

Caroline and Ned Conway probe the Gosnold Pond guzzle in advance of BUCKRAMMER's exit.

out of the river bottom and stored it on deck. Near the exit of the channel, Caroline used our boathook to snag the fender-marked kedge line. She then hand-over-handed it aboard as the outboard kicked us forward; piece of cake.

Out of the shallows, we lowered the centerboard, hoisted sail and pointed BUCKRAMMER home. Thank you Captain Jeremy B. Whitney. Thank you, thank you, and thank you.

Epilogue

In the years since Jeremy Whitney drafted his remarkable *Gunkholing Guide to Buzzard's Bay*, many catboaters have enjoyed the manuscript and safely followed its directions. Succumbing to overwhelming demand, the editorial board of the Catboat Association finally relented and published the work. You will find it in *The Bulletin* of the Catboat Association, Number 120, Fall 1999, pp. 20–28. This issue is available directly from the Catboat Association. Don't sail Buzzard's Bay without it.

8

—⟨∿∿⟩—

Restless James
of Swan Pond

"We've seen a ghost! We've seen a ghost! We've seen a ghost."

All three Conway children, their faces ghost-white themselves, screamed as they pulled alongside in SPLINTER, clambered into BUCKRAMMER's cockpit and cowered.

My wife Chris and I had been enjoying a lazy early morning of breakfasting, reading and lazing around in a couple of hammocks hung off the boat's 32-foot main boom. Key words, *had* been enjoying.

"Whoa! Whoa everyone," Chris pleaded. "You've obviously had a good scare but how could ghosts be involved? It's broad daylight."

The whole adventure had begun three days earlier as we set sail from our summer base in Westport. We had selected a prime, weeklong slice of July as our traditional family boating vacation time. This year's trip would include, as Chris liked to taunt, a "Roots" excursion. I had spent many of my early summers as a child in West Dennis, Massachusetts. It was here that my brothers and I were given out first boat, an 8-foot plywood pram. With this little yacht, from our base on the Swan Pond River, we had explored every nook and cranny of the south coast of the Cape from Hyannis to Harwich. This year's Conway Cruise would revisit this hallowed, time-honored and overdeveloped chunk of shoreline.

Chris and most (maybe all) of the family had voted for our more traditional Elizabeth Islands-Martha's Vineyard-Nantucket triangular tour. I had strongly suggested substituting the West Dennis-to-Harwichport component for Nantucket. After considerable pleading, whining and bribing, I got "the fam" to relent.

Over the past few days we had journeyed through the Elizabeth Islands (Cuttyhunk and Hadley Harbor on this run) and had now made our way to the Dogfish Bar region of West Dennis. Here we would explore the Bass River, the Swan Pond River and the Herring Rivers, roughly in that order.

Our approach to the Bass River had been marred with an attack by a squadron of jet skiers. (Chris gave me that "I told you so, Mr. Roots Trip" look.) So we decided to forgo that inlet and diverted to my old haunt, the aforementioned and peaceful guzzle know as the Swan Pond River. Normally even a boat with the 2-foot draft of BUCKRAMMER would have trouble entering the "Swan," but luck was with us in the guise of an astronomically high flood tide. As a result, with a few feet of water to spare, we slipped across the bar around noontime and into the tight but excellent anchorages within the saltmarshes of West Dennis.

West Dennis offers some of the nicest swimming on the Cape, with July water temperatures often approaching a tropical 75 to 80 degrees. This summer had been kinder than usual to the bathers. BUCKRAMMER's digital temperature gauge read a constant 78 degrees on our approach to the Swan Pond River and an unbelievable 82 degrees in the guzzle itself. Yum!

We planned to spend a day exploring the area, swimming and relaxing. From the river we could also row the dinghy a few hundred yards upstream to a very nice seafood restaurant, appropriately named the Swan Pond River Fish

Market; we could walk into the village of West Dennis, which offered a reasonable collection of food, liquor, and antique and book shops; and, more importantly, we could journey along South Village and Lower County Roads to the summerhouses where I stayed in the 1950s and 1960s, where I could regale the troops with a number of "Roots" tales. Ah, the memories! My family opted for swimming, eating and shopping in roughly that order. I took a mostly solo trip down memory lane.

That night, after a filling restaurant dinner of fried haddock and Ipswich clams, we plodded back to the boat and plopped onto the cushions of BUCKRAMMER's cockpit to digest things for a while. As the deep purple of dusk closed in, it only seemed appropriate (groan) to dig out a few roots stories about the area. One that seemed to gain more attention than the other tales involved my brothers' and my fas-

BUCKRAMMER enters the Swam Pond River, off West Dennis, Massachusetts in search of the haunted cemetery.

cination with an old family farm that had been abandoned near our summer cottage on South Village Road. My farm story went something like this:

"In an era of million dollar Cape Cod properties, it's hard to imagine that as recently as the 1950s and 1960s, Cape Cod was littered with abandoned properties that could be purchased by anyone willing to pay the outstanding tax bill. One of these properties, a parcel of about twenty acres, was located about a quarter mile from where we were currently anchored. The homestead comprised a three-story, six-bedroom farmhouse and a number of outbuildings, including a chicken coop, a barn and a horse corral. Several abandoned 1930s-looking cars and trucks were thrown in for good measure. There was also a tiny cemetery containing the remains of the Baker family: Calvin (the father), Polly (the mother) and James (a son). With the family plot as a guide, my brothers and I knew this farmstead as The Bakers' Place."

I continued: "As pre-teens, my brothers and I used The Bakers' Place as our own personal playground. We would explore the house—legend said there was a treasure—pretend to drive the Bonnie and Clyde-style cars and trucks, play hide-and-seek with friends all over the property and just plain have fun. To make everything copacetic, every now and then we would pay our respects to the Baker family by leaving flowers picked from the rose bushes or daisy clusters that covered the grounds around the house.

"One summer, an itinerant sea captain–looking hobo we nicknamed "Cap'n Peleg" moved into the dining room on the first floor of the house. We stumbled on old Peleg by accident one day when we literally tripped over him where he was snoozing on an old mattress on the floor. From that first encounter onward, Peleg scared the hell out of us (we probably scared him as much or more). We played cat and mouse with the crafty hobo all summer long.

"One year we came down for the season only to discover that the Town of West Dennis had taken it upon itself to dynamite the house as a safety hazard. In short order a developer acquired the property and built a number of "year-round" homes. This event, perhaps more than any other, delineated the end of my childhood, at least in my mind."

My son Ned was the first to ask a question that had popped into everyone's mind. "Whatever happened to the family cemetery?"

"Beats me!" I replied. "Rumor had it that the Town had disinterred the remains, moved them and reinterred them in the main cemetery. But maybe the plot is still just sitting there."

Caroline winced. "Dad, I can't believe that the people in those new houses would allow an old, family cemetery to remain in their backyards. That would be weird."

"You're probably right," I replied. "But there *is* one way to determine what happened. Let's pay a visit."

This seemed to catch the interest of all of the Conway kids. Chris, on the other hand, was a bit concerned.

"Oh great! I can just see it now. Grown man and children arrested for trespassing in West Dennis. Film at 11:00."

Abby stepped in. "Mom, before you pull the plug on what could be the most interesting part of our vacation, I've got a plan. Why don't Ned, Caroline and I head over early tomorrow morning and check out the place? We're just kids and can always claim that we got lost or something else equally lame. The police wouldn't throw such innocents into the pokey. And if they did, you could bail us out."

Chris looked the look that only a disapproving mother can conjure. I, on the other hand, was intrigued. "It does sound like a plan, hon."

So it was that the Conway Baker Expedition came into existence. Long before Chris and I woke up the following day, the CBE members had dressed, rowed ashore and headed out. All of which brings us back to:

"We've seen a ghost! We've seen a ghost! We've seen a ghost." Abby was the first to settle down enough to tell the tale.

As agreed last night, the CBE members had dressed and pulled out just a tad after dawn. They rowed up the river to the landmarks that I had told them defined the old Baker property. There they beached the SPLINTER and crossed over to the "new" houses that comprise the development. Between two of the houses, roughly in the direction of the old family plot, someone had laid out a path defined by two rows of beach cobblestones. They walked between the stones and soon found themselves in a clump of vines and brambles and scrub pines. Pushing the weeds aside, they came face-to-face with the remains of the Baker cemetery. It was surrounded by an iron-pipe fence supported by granite corner posts.

Abby continued. "We stepped over the fence and into the plot. The tombstone of Calvin and Polly was tipped over so we could only see the words 'Mother' and 'Father.' We decided to tip it back onto its stand. Once we did that, we could clearly read the names and dates. Geez Dad, it was just like you described."

Ned, now recovered enough to speak intelligibly, chimed in. "That's when we heard the music."

"Music?" Chris asked.

"Yeah," Ned replied, "music that sounded like someone playing the violin very poorly and at a high pitch. It seemed all around us at first, then we noticed that it was coming from the rear, right corner of the cemetery. We were creeped out!"

"That was the ghost?" I teased. "Some violin music?"

Caroline piped up. "Daaaad! What do you take us for? No, the violin music was weird but that's not what scared us. We saw another stone so we figured that must be the son, James. As we turned away from the Calvin and Polly tombstone and headed toward James's stone, the violin music got louder and his tombstone began to rock back and forth! It was as if James was trying to climb out of his casket. I think we even heard the wooden lid of his box banging. THAT is what made us run back to SPLINTER and race back here. THAT is why we need to leave *right now*. James was absolutely, positively coming to get us. His spirit is clearly on the prowl." All of the kids nodded in agreement.

Chris and I looked at one another and, even though we were bathed in bright morning sunshine and the temperature was in the 80s, our blood ran a tad cold.

"Well, we have to go back." All of us turned to look at Chris as she made this pronouncement. We all thought she had slipped a crown washer or two.

I squirmed. "Er, why would you want to put us into harm's way?"

"Harm's way, bah!" Chris rejoined. "There must be a logical explanation, and we've got to find out what it is."

Abby spoke for the CBE members. "Tell you what, Mom, Dad. We kids have had quite enough excitement for one morning. Why don't you two go back and let us know what you find?"

"OK fraidy cats," Chris scolded. "But don't blame us when you regret not having had the curiosity to learn the truth. 'The Truth Is Out There,' you know." Chris turned and looked at me. "Ready?"

I swallowed hard, believing that I was about to step into an episode of the *X-Files*. "Sure?"

Within a half hour Chris and I stood at the fence surrounding the grave site. We stepped into the plot and scanned around. My first reaction was one of great sadness. Time (and probably vandals) had not been kind to the little family cemetery. The iron fence was missing more rails than there were good rails. Rubbish and junk, including pieces of one of the old cars, were strewn about everywhere. I began to feel angry that this poor little piece of sacred ground had been neglected for so long. I thought of the old saying "There but for the grace of God go I."

Chris and I continued to look around. Just as the kids had told us, the headstone of Calvin and Polly was now back on its perch. James's stone was there in the back. Chris motioned me forward.

As I approached James's grave I'll be damned if bad violin music didn't begin to play. Then, as if on cue, the headstone began to rock back and forth slowly. Chris and I felt our blood curdling but we stood our ground.

The music and the rocking stopped.

Feeling a bit emboldened, I took a few steps toward James's stone. Once again the music began and the rocking commenced. Chris came up behind me and touched my arm. I must have jumped 50 feet in the air if it were an inch.

"Don't do that! Gawd, you almost gave me heart failure."

"Sorry, but I wanted to tell you that I think I've figured this out."

With me cautiously in tow, Chris walked over to the stone and pointed. One eye open, one shut, I peered over the headstone. "Son of a gun."

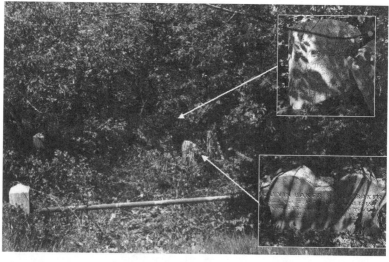

Though abandoned to nature, the Baker-family plot still hosts an "active" set of residents. (Top inset) Headstone of son James T. Baker. (Bottom inset) Headstone of both Calvin (father) and Polly (mother) Baker.

The Mystery Solved?

"Wait a minute, wait a minute. You can't stop there." Ned was clearly miffed.

Back on BUCKRAMMER we had told the kids the story of our graveyard adventure but stopped short of revealing the solution to the ghostly mystery.

"Well smarty pants people, you chose not to go back. So I'm afraid that you'll never know the answer to the riddle." Chris can be really nasty if she wants to.

Fortunately neither one of us is especially good at keeping a juicy secret.

"OK, OK, here's what we found." Chris and I tag-teamed the answer.

"We saw exactly the same scene as you did and we almost ran like the proverbial "bats out of hell" as well. But we lingered just a few seconds longer and that was all it took for Mom to notice the tree."

"The tree?"

"Yup! Over the years a skinny little scrub pine has grown up through James's resting place. The tree displaced the headstone such that the stone now rubs against the edge of one of the remaining gravesite railings. As the wind blows the upper branches of the tree and the tree sways to and fro, a couple of things happen. First, the back-and-forth motion of the tree causes the tombstone to rock back and forth as well. Second, the rocking tombstone rubs the rail in such a way as to make the violin noise, sort of like someone dragging fingernails along a chalkboard. That one little tree causes both the rocking and the music. Mystery solved."

The kids just sat there in the sunny cockpit pondering the explanation to an event that, just a few hours earlier, had nearly frightened them to death. Almost simultaneously they sighed sheepishly. "Well waddayaknow!" The remainder of our visit to West Dennis went uneventfully.

On the final leg of our journey, on our way over to

Martha's Vineyard, Ned joined me at the wheel. "Dad, I've been thinking about the solution to our ghostly experience. Everything makes sense except for one thing. Abby, Caroline and I clearly heard the violin music *before* we saw the headstone rocking. From your description, that's what you and Mom observed as well. How do you 'splain that with your tree theory big guy?"

I looked down at Ned and puzzled his question a bit. "Ah well, er, I'm . . . Hmmm." A cold shiver went down my spine as I just shrugged and headed south.

Epilogue

A year or so after this experience, we bumped into a friend of a friend who had spoken with the owner of one of the homes that abuts the Baker family plot. He reported that the homeowner had had a creepy experience of his own. As the story goes, one stormy night, with each lightning flash, the wife of the homeowner noticed something white glistening in the old plot. The next day, at his wife's insistence, the man went over to examine the graves. On top of James Baker's grave he found some leg or arm bones and what he believed was one of the side handles to James's coffin. The man reburied the bones but kept the handle to show his wife. They both believe that the little pine tree is responsible for pushing both the bones and the handle to the surface. Whatever the case, the handle now graces the mantelpiece of their home. There but for the grace of God *go us all*?

9

—⟨∞⟩—

Search for the
Jumping Sandbar

"Maybe you, your sister and the boys should wait until to-morrow morning?" My mother looked more worried than usual. "It's almost 10:00 Saturday night!"

"Nope! We promised the kids an overnighter, and an overnighter they shall have."

My parents, my youngest sister, Rosalyn, and her two boys, Cole (age nine) and Jack (age four), had come to Westport from their home in California for a week of summer vacation with us. For months in advance of their visit, I had been promising the kids that we would have an overnighter on the BUCKRAMMER. Due to a scheduling snag with my next weekend (an unanticipated business trip), this weekend evening would be the last chance to keep my word.

As is always the case when guests visit us in Westport, we had filled the day with too many activities, including an extended family breakfast, visits to a few antique shops, a four-hour-plus-lunch stay at the beach and then dinner, followed by several hours of square dancing at the neighborhood church hall. Though the grown-ups had almost reached their "fun quotient," Cole and Jack were still full of energy and rearing to go.

"Come on," I pleaded. "The boys are ready, the boat is ready, it's a beautiful, sultry night and the magic of summer surrounds us."

Rosalyn rolled her eyes but relented. "OK, but we do this safely and calmly, right?"

"Absolutely!" I replied.

Cole and Jack nodded in violent agreement. My mother and father, however, decided that they had had enough adventure for the day. My dad said, "You know that I'd love to go, but *your mother* insists that we spend the night in that comfortable bed in your guest room here on dry land. Tell you what, though, we'll meet you for breakfast on your catboat, if you don't mind."

I said that I didn't mind at all. So, with everything settled, we quickly assembled sleeping bags, pillows, foodstuffs and other essentials, loaded up our old Suburban (affectionately known in our family as "The Meat Wagon") and drove down to the dinghy dock at Slaight's Wharf. Everyone was issued a life jacket and, after a bit of fussing, we all slipped them on and buckled up. The four of us then formed a human chain and hand-over-handed the supplies from the Meat Wagon down the gangplank to our "shuttle craft," the SPLINTER.

Finally around 11:00 P.M. we finished loading up. I got into SPLINTER first and took the center (rowing) seat. Rosalyn and Jack followed and sat in the rear of the boat. Cole positioned himself in the bow. On my "cast off" command, Cole uncleated the painter; I gave our vessel a little nudge, mounted the oars in the oar horns and rowed the boating party into the inky brine. (In all truthfulness, with Slaight's Wharf surrounded by well-lit homes, marinas and restaurants, the brine was more winky and blinky than inky.)

"Look! The water is on fire!" Jack yelled. Cole and Rosalyn shifted around to see and the boat tipped a touch to port.

"Whoa, cowboys!" I barked. "Everyone settle down; no quick movements and I'll explain." The crew complied.

I continued. "This time of year, around late July, a harmless type of jellyfish called the ctenophore"—pronounced "ten-a-four," each about the size of a walnut, move into the waters of the Westport River. You can hardly see them in the daytime but if you poke them with an oar at night, they react by lighting up like a Christmas tree bulb underwater." As I said this one of the oars smacked a cluster of the little creatures and they gave us a grand show.

"Uncle John, let me try," Jack demanded.

"OK. Put your hands on top of my hands on the oars and help me row. I bet we'll hit a bunch."

Jack did so and, sure enough, the water around SPLINTER came alive with phosphorescence. After a few dozen strokes, I asked Cole if he wanted to try. He nodded, yes, so I switched the oars to the forward set of horns and let him have a whack at the comb jellies. After another dozen strikes, I moved the oars back into their original position and shifted into rowing overdrive. SPLINTER would soon leave Slaight's Inlet and enter the mainstream of the Westport River's outgoing current. To counter this force, I would need all of the available oar power.

"Look behind us!" Cole pointed astern. "SPLINTER looks like a starship flying at hyperspeed." Sure enough, the accelerated rowing pushed a great number of luminescent animals behind us. Together the creatures produced a dazzling display that gave SPLINTER the appearance of a rocket ship using star-drive propulsion. Very cool!

Before long our star-shuttle arrived alongside the mother ship BUCKRAMMER. After warning my passengers to keep their hands and bodies inside of SPLINTER, I held on to our big boat's rubrail and directed Rosalyn and the kids to climb aboard in the reverse order that they had boarded the dinghy.

Hokey as it sounds, there *is* something magical about staying aboard an old wooden boat in harbor on a grand summer's evening. The creak and smell of the pine-tarred wood, the caress of the gentle breeze, the easy-on-the eyes illumination of the oil lamps, the gurgle of water on cedar, the starlight and moonlight—all these experiences combine to great effect.

I took the cabin door keys from their secret hiding place and handed them to Rosalyn. She unlocked the louvers, latched the doors open, went below and lit the lamps. While she and the boys prepared their bunks for sleeping, I restocked the galley with provisions.

Pulling a pair of binoculars from their holder near the coal stove, I asked. "Anyone interested in looking for planets?" No one answered. As I began to ask again I shot a glance toward the bunks. Rosalyn, Cole and Jack, snug in their sleeping bags but still in their life jackets, were already sound asleep.

I quietly snuffed the wicks, grabbed a blanket and pillow for myself and came up on deck. I closed and secured the cabin doors to prevent any potential sleepwalking lads from taking an unexpected night swim. Then I lay down on the cockpit's starboard seat, propped a pillow under my head, pulled up the blanket and, after counting four falling stars, one for each of us aboard, dozed off.

A Baited Breakfast

"Uncle John, Uncle John. It's fish'n time."

Jack delivered my wake-up call. He had obviously discovered one of the two fishing rod/reel combos stored below and had figured out how to open the cabin doors. Now, gear in hand, he hopped around in the cockpit like a flea on a hot griddle.

I cracked open my eyes and snuck a peek at my watch: 4:50 A.M. Ouch!

"OK, Jack. Let's set you up."

The Conway clan is not really "into" fishing. So BUCK-RAMMER's rods are kept on board for comic relief more than anything else. At 4:50 in the morning, however, even this humor can elude a body. Nevertheless, I broke out the tackle box, snapped on one of the two lures within, cast the line out into the river 5 yards or so and handed the rig to my nephew. He eagerly took hold with a viselike grip.

"Just keep jigging the line like this," I explained as if I knew what to do.

Jack nodded. "Right Uncle John, right Uncle John. Just like those guys."

"Those guys?"

It was only then that I looked up and noticed that we were surrounded by a flotilla of little motorboats, each containing one to four fishermen jigging their own lines. I waved to the boat nearest to us. The fishermen within waved back. Just as I was about to yell over to them to ask what they were fishing for, and what lure or bait they were using, it dawned on me that this act might awaken the others. I decided instead to reposition myself on the cockpit seat, pillow underhead and blanket overhead, save for one eye to keep on Jack.

"Uncle John, Uncle John! I think I've got a whale."

I bolted from a half-doze and jumped to Jack's side. Sure enough, something had "struck," for his rod twitched and bent with action; time now 5:08 A.M.

Jack and I reeled in the great beast only to discover a basketball-sized clump of seaweed and eelgrass.

"Uncle John, Uncle John! Guess we caught the wrong thing."

I agreed. "Yup! Let's put 'er back and try again, eh?"

For the next couple hours the process repeated itself to the point where the little guy had "catch'd" all of the weeds that the Westport River had generated during this summer or next. However, Jack's determination to catch a fish remained undaunted throughout. Not bad for a little guy. Maybe he had inherited the fisherman's genes from his dad. I'd have to ask Rosalyn about Bill's hobbies.

Round about 7:00 A.M. Cole emerged from the cabin. He spied Jack in action and, naturally, wanted a fishing rod of his own. I got him set up with the other rig, and both brothers continued the process of scouring the river of seaweed.

Little did we know that one of the fishermen, anchored off to our starboard, had observed first Jack's and then both boys' attempts at landing the big one. Now he started his outboard, motored over and pulled alongside.

"Looks like you've had a bad run this fine morn," he commented.

A bit startled, Jack, Cole and I shrugged in agreement.

"Name's Bob Teixeira but most call me the Porta-Gea. Who might you all be?"

My nephews and I introduced ourselves to a man who looked like the proverbial "Old Man of the Sea" in the flesh.

Teixeira tossed us a plastic container and continued, "Here, take these frozen sea clams. You can catch anything in this river with these grubbers. Gar-Ron-Teed! Why, I bet you'll have fish for breakfast. Have a good one."

With that, the Porta-Gea gunned his engine and scooted away downriver. The boys and I were still a bit bewildered by this stranger's appearance and generosity.

Cole Conway casts for a fishy breakfast off of Westport Point.

"Hey Uncle John! What are we waiting for?" Cole was the first in line for a bait load.

After removing the lures and replacing them with snelled hooks and lead sinkers, we baited up and cast our rigs upon the waters. Within seconds fish hit both lines.

"I've got a whale, I've got a whale!" Now an expert, Jack *knew* that this was no seaweed attack.

"I think I've got something too," Cole reported.

Dumbfounded, I replied, "Well for goodness sake, reel them in boys, reel 'em in."

Amazingly, within thirty minutes, Jack and Cole had filled a five-gallon pail with about fifteen "shiner blues," a mackerel-like kind of juvenile bluefish (I think) suitable for pan or grill.

"What did I miss? What did I miss?" Rosalyn stuck her head through the doghouse roof. The boys raced to her and described the situation. Glad for the boys' success but also glad that Uncle John had let her sleep, Rosalyn took it all in and then replied, "So! Anyone want fish for breakfast?"

To a man, the rest of us yelled a resounding "Yuck!" Maybe the fishing gene had not infected my nephews after all.

A Quick Jump

Hunger now took the driver's seat. We cleaned and stowed the fishing tackle, and then Rosalyn shooshed the boys below to get them washed up and changed into bathing suits. In the interim, my parents appeared on the dock and I rowed them over to BUCKRAMMER. When everyone was settled, my dad and I fired the griddle and served up a breakfast of blueberry pancakes and Canadian bacon chased with fresh-squeezed orange juice. I'm sure we all felt that blueberries beat bluefish for breakfast any day.

My mother and Rosalyn volunteered to clean up breakfast while my father and I prepared the boat for the day's excursion. With everything shipshape I called everyone into the cockpit to explain the day's events.

"Today we hunt for the Jumping Sandbar. We—"

Jack interrupted, " 'Scuse me, 'scuse me, Uncle John. How can a sandbar jump?"

Cole gave Jack a poke. "Don't interrupt Uncle John. You see, the sandbar, er, um, well . . . Yeah, Uncle John, how can a sandbar jump?"

"The sandbar doesn't jump, the people do. See?" I explained. But the blank expressions on the folks' faces suggested that I needed to take things from the top.

"OK! Let me start over. Back in the olden days, when your cousins Abby, Ned and Caroline were your age, the Westport River did not look like it does now. In those times, the channels and mudflats and sandbars were located in different places underwater. In 1991, Hurricane Bob changed everything in a single afternoon. All of our favorite places to sail and dig for clams and swim and skin-dive were relocated when the terrible winds and waters of the hurricane moved most of the bottom of the river around." My audience continued to pay attention, so I continued.

"One of our favorite spots was a tidal island we nicknamed 'The Jumping Sandbar.' At low tide, a large sandbar would emerge from beneath the water and become dry land for a few hours. At one end of the bar, Nature had formed what scientists call a 'harbor hole': a deep whirlpool of water formed by the action of the river currents swirling around the marshes and clam flats."

Cole barged in. "So where does the jumping part come in?"

Not missing a beat on his older brother, Jack piped up, "Don't interrupt Uncle John, Cole you big pookie boy." Rosalyn calmed the situation before it turned nuclear, and I resumed the tale.

"On an outgoing low tide, the warm, upriver water would gush through and swirl around in the hole on its way to the ocean. The combination of the deep bottom and hot water provided a wonderful place to swim. Best of all, the unique formation of the sandbar also made the hole the *greatest* place to dive."

It was Rosalyn's turn to interrupt. "What do you mean?" she said.

I pressed on. "You would not think it possible with flowing water and a sandy shore, but at the exact spot where the sandbar and hole met, the bottom abruptly dropped almost straight down to a depth of 15 feet or so. This meant that a swimmer could stand on the edge of the sandbar and then jackknife into the 80-degree water without hitting the bottom. It was just like taking a plunge off the high-dive at a swimming pool. Better yet, a diver could walk back from the hole about 100 feet, then turn, run his or her heart out and take a flying leap into the thing. The practice of taking leaps into the hole gave rise to the name, Jumping Sandbar."

"So the hurricane destroyed the hole?" my mother asked.

"Unfortunately, yes," I replied. "Hurricane Bob washed the Jumping Sandbar out to sea, swimming hole and all. Ever since then we have combed the entire river in vain, hoping to discover a new jumping sandbar and harbor hole. Now we think that we have found one and that's where we are going today. Does everyone want to come?"

Our cockpit chorus rose up with a resounding "YES!" and five minutes later BUCKRAMMER slipped away from her mooring, SPLINTER in tow, and headed down river toward what we all hoped would be the New Jumping Sandbar.

Experience, both good and bad, with my own gang over the years has given me some understanding of how to introduce kids to the pleasures of boating. The key lies in trying not to overdo things in a burst of adult enthusiasm for the sport. Take boating with little people (and perhaps spouses as well) in small bites that leave everyone wanting for more. When I learned that my sister and her children had planned a vacation with us, including an overnight boating trip, my first inclination was to take the whole gang to Cuttyhunk Island and back, an offshore round-trip of about 24 miles. Fortunately, experience prevailed and I scaled things down to a river excursion of 3 miles round-trip. This way, if anyone got scared or seasick or cranky, we would never be more than a few minutes from home.

My smaller-is-beautiful strategy seemed to pay off when, ten minutes away from our destination, both Cole and Jack spoke the dreaded words, "Are we there yet?" Turns out, we were!

"Anchors away!"

Just across from Corey's Island on the western end of what the charts call Grand Island (really just a big marsh), BUCKRAMMER hove to and dropped the hook in about six feet of clear river water. If my son Ned's scouting reports from earlier in the week were correct, the eastern end of the sandbar now just emerging to the north would become our new, ultimate swim'n hole.

Holy Cows and Other Stunts

Once we anchored and settled in, the ladies offered to pack a lunch while the rest of us went ashore to reconnoiter. I took my customary position at the oars, my dad and Jack sat in the stern and Cole served as our figurehead. After a short pull, SPLINTER beached on the sandbar and everyone got out and waded ashore. In the twenty minutes it had taken us to anchor BUCKRAMMER and row in, the sandbar had fully emerged and we had "made land" around the middle of the pseudo-island. This placed us about 200 yards from the supposedly "holy" place. The scouting party made a dash along the beach toward the sandbar's eastern end. The boys arrived first but stopped shy of the water. My dad and I soon caught up. The spot looked promising.

"Whadayathink?" My dad offered.

"Only one way to find out," I said. "Let's throw in a small child and see what happens."

All of the blood drained from Jack's and Cole's upper bodies. Quick as a flash they ran for their lives back toward SPLINTER. My dad and I nearly split our sides laughing.

I yelled after them, "Just kidding! Come on back you big fraidy cats."

The boys stopped their run and turned to eye us from afar but refused to come any closer. There was only one thing to do. I took off my shirt, walked to the end of the sandbar and stepped gingerly into the watery void. Sploosh! I found myself in a deep pool of very warm water. For the next few minutes, I swam around in the hole to determine its dimensions and to see if it contained any hazards, such as hidden rocks or nasty, waterlogged tree stumps. From this exercise I discovered that the hole measured about 50 feet wide by 75 feet long by about 15 feet deep and that it

The author's parents, nephews and sister "on the brink" of the Jumping Sandbar. (L/R) John, Sr, (father), Doris (mother), Cole and Jack (nephews), and Rosalyn (sister).

seemed clear of natural obstructions or debris. After a three-year search, we had indeed found a New Jumping Sandbar.

"Last one in's a rotten egg," I yelled to my dad.

With reckless abandon, the old-timer executed a graceful dive into the heart of the hole. He surfaced with the biggest smile I had seen on him in decades.

"Wow! This is sublime."

One after the other, my dad and I jumped into the water, exited and jumped in again. After about five minutes of this, it dawned on us that my nephews were still standing midway between the dinghy and the hole.

I yelled, "Come on guys! The water is grrrrrrr . . . ate!"

With their own form of reckless abandon, the life-jacketed lads followed the old geezers into the embrace of the watery playpen.

We all whooped it up until, after about thirty minutes, the air horn on BUCKRAMMER went off. I looked over at the boat to see my mother and sister waving at us for a ride.

"Oops!"

"Did we forget something?" My mother looked a touch peeved as I pulled SPLINTER alongside BUCKRAMMER.

"Er, sorry Mom. We got a little carried away." I spied the fully packed cooler chest. "Oh, looks like you've built a great lunch."

"Don't change the subject, sonny boy. Just get us over to the beach so that we can join in the fun."

"Yes, ma'am," I squeaked.

Soon the entire party was encamped on the little island. My mother and sister had packed a deli's load of sandwiches, chips, salsa, cookies and cold drinks. And we swam and drank and laughed and played the late morning and early afternoon away.

My dad and I, lifelong experts at swimming hole gymnastics, took it upon ourselves to instruct the lesser mortals on the high art of hole jumping. In short order we had passed on to our attentive pupils such legendary jumps as

The Geronimo, The Turn Around Wave Bye-Bye, The Atomic Cannonball, The Wile E. Coyote, and the seldom performed, Holy Cow (don't ask!).

Around 1:00 the tide turned and by 3:00 our happy little world, like some poor man's Atlantis, began to slip beneath the waves. The ladies and the remains of lunch went back to the BUCKRAMMER first. Jack, Cole and my dad went last. We stored everything away, fired up the old diesel, weighed anchor and headed home.

Originally billed as an overnight event for a couple of kids and their mom, the excursion had turned into one of the most satisfying and enjoyable days of our many catboat summers.

10

—◦◦◦—

Return to
Uncle Charlie's

"Well Dad, that little twig of a bridge is the only thing separating BUCKRAMMER from her bassinet and you and the fam from some "cold ones" and dinner. I suggest that you hail the operator and get him to open it." Abby's eyes toggled back and forth between the Oyster Harbor drawbridge and my face.

"Cold ones?" I reprimanded.

"Sure! You know, lemonade, soda pop, schtuff like that." Abby said with a wink.

I unclipped the mike from its holder above the VHF radio and called the bridgemaster. As the old span shuddered, lifted and allowed us to pass, it seemed to welcome us home into another time and place.

For years I had promised that "some day" I would sail BUCKRAMMER back to the Crosby Yacht Yard, in historic Osterville on Cape Cod, as another sort of "Roots" trip. But as each season came and went, the 50-plus-mile journey seemed to slip ever lower on the to-do list. With so many nooks and crannies to explore in Buzzard's Bay, and with so little time to enjoy them, Osterville floated just over the edge of "visitability."

Several events pushed the trip back onto the docket. The first occurred when David Crosby, a retired Cape Cod school-teacher with a direct bloodline to the legendary catboat builders, decided to write to me. He had read one of my BUCKRAMMER tales in the magazine *Messing About In Boats* and wrote to say how much he enjoyed it. I wrote back, thanked him and asked if he had any documentation pertaining to Charles Crosby, our boat's builder. Within days, I received a note: "John: Enclosed find the family tree of the boatbuilding Crosbys of Osterville. Barbara should be given credit for all of the research—which is continuing in much greater detail to cover the entire Crosby family—quite a chore."

From this simple beginning, over a series of months, David and his wife Barbara sent a wealth of genealogical, historical and anecdotal information about "Uncle Charlie." In one letter Dave wrote, "oh by the way, Uncle Charlie's North Shop boathouse, the place where he built your cat-boat, still stands in all of its glory. You really should pay it a visit while you can."

I knew that the Crosby Yacht Yard still built the occasional boat (Stripers, small tugs, yacht club tenders and a Wianno Senior now and then), but I was dumbfounded to learn that Charles Crosby's waterfront boatbuilding shed could have survived over the ninety-plus years since BUCK-RAMMER slipped her ways.

The second event occurred in a bookshop. Since becoming BUCKRAMMER's caretaker, I have purchased and read all manner of antique boating books and magazines. These publications, written when the gaff-rigged wooden boat was the norm among small craft, provide wonderful guidance and insight into the history, sailing techniques and mainte-nance programs of wooden boats of BUCKRAMMER's vintage. Over the years, the Brattle Book Shop on West Street in Boston has served as a reliable source for my collection. Pro-prietor Ken Gloss, continuing in the tradition of his father George Gloss (a literary mentor to many of us who grew up

in Boston in the 1950s and 1960s), stocks a constantly churn-
ing collection of "previously owned" items ranging from
maps and periodicals to books and curios.

On one of my visits there, during the time that I was cor-
responding with David and Barbara, I chanced upon a
bound volume of *The Rudder* magazine, probably the most
widely read of the pre–World War II boating monthlies. The
2-inch-thick book included issues covering the period from
January to December 1906. I took the work from the display
shelf and casually thumbed through the pages, searching for
anything of value to my "catboat cause." By the most
serendipitous of chances, my page-turning brought me to an
article April 1906 (volume 17) entitled "A Catboat Sailor's
Yarn," by Winfield M. Thompson.

In Thompson's own words, the story provides "a simple
tale of how an ordinary amateur . . . bought a cruising, Cape
Cod cat, fitted her out and managed her for a season." More
remarkably, Boston-based Thompson "went to Osterville,
the home of the Cape Cod cat, to have a look at the famous
Crosby shops and their current products." Over fourteen,
copiously illustrated pages, Thompson describes how he examined, bought, outfitted and learned to sail a Crosby catboat named TWISTER just a few years before BUCKRAMMER'S
construction. Unbelievable!

The chance discovery of this article remains, to this day,
one of the most remarkable coincidences of my catboat experience. Feeling as if I had discovered the Rosetta Stone, I
bought the book and raced home.

In the comfort of my home office, I read the story and
examined the photos and drawings in detail. I was a touch
disappointed to learn that Charles Crosby's brother, Daniel,
built the boat described in *The Rudder*. However, by corre-
lating the data provided by David and Barbara with that revealed in the 1906 article, I determined that several photos
in the article showed Uncle Charlie's North Shop. "So that's
where the old bucket was built," I mused.

The "yarn" also provided an incredible glimpse into the interior layout of an early-twentieth-century Crosby catboat. As described in the Appendices below, we have used this layout as a guide during our continuing restoration of BUCK-RAMMER.

Put Osterville on the List

These revelations considerably sharpened our interest in a trip to Osterville. Even my better half, Chris, not one to take long sailing trips lightly, thought that the gods had beckoned us to BUCKRAMMER's birthplace.

"It would be neat to see how much of the original boat-shop remains and to talk with the present owner of the yard," Chris commented. "I also hear that the town of Osterville has a lot to offer with quaint old shops, museums and restaurants. We should plan a trip this summer. Don't you think?" Who was I to disagree?

A window of weather, tide, and family schedule opened late in July. We loaded up for an extended weekend and set off, spirits high. Our course would take our gang to Hadley Harbor in the Elizabeth Islands by lunchtime and then on to Osterville by dinner.

The first leg of the journey, enhanced by a very favorable southwest wind that gave us "downhill" sailing almost all of the way to Hadley, went without incident. Most visitors rank Hadley Harbor as one of the most tranquil, picturesque locations in New England. The harbor lies at the northern extremity of the private portions of the Elizabeth Islands owned and managed by the extended Forbes family. The Forbeses allow boaters to anchor in the extended reaches of the harbor, but do not allow shore visits without permission. Nevertheless, the unspoiled, natural beauty of the place attracts thousands of boaters passing through Buzzard's Bay each year.

With Chris on board, the family was treated to a gourmet lunch of homemade egg-salad and tomato sandwiches on French bread with hand-cut coleslaw and fresh-brewed mint ice tea (the mint from Chris's own garden!). Mom topped off the feast by passing around a plate of double-chocolate, pecan brownies.

After cleaning up the lunch things, we yanked the hook, started Red, Jr. and nosed out into Wood's Hole. "The Hole" can be a tricky place when conditions work against you, but on this glorious day Nature offered us a harmonious passage. Once through the channel, BUCKRAMMER hugged the Falmouth coast of Cape Cod, nudged along by sultry, moderate winds typical for these waters in late July.

"Is that a bump in the ocean?" Caroline, our resident worrywart, pointed out an interesting phenomenon off our port bow. Indeed, the otherwise flat seas were disrupted by a tennis court–sized mound of water about a foot higher than the surrounding ocean. Curious as to what we saw, I asked Caroline to get a GPS fix and then consult the navigation charts. After a bit of fussing, Caroline reported, "Looks like a current boil over an old shipwreck. Here, take a look."

One glance at the chart and it hit me like a dope slap. "Of course! It's the PORT HUNTER," I blurted.

My shout knocked the rest of the family out of their post-lunch doze. I winced. "Sorry, but we're about to pass close to a shipwreck that I scuba dived on in my college days." Everyone, but Caroline, shrugged and went back to sleep.

Caroline inquired, "The PORT HUNTER?"

I bit. "Yup! She's an intact, 380-foot freighter that collided with the tugboat COVINGTON and sank here on the Hedge Fence Shoal way back in November of 1918. The 4,000-ton ship carried a mixed cargo of war supplies, industrial machinery, chemicals and dry goods. The steamer lies at a severe angle, with her bow end in 20 feet of water and her stern end in 85 feet or so. She makes a great dive."

"Will we hit the ship or the shoal?" A wide-eyed Caroline twitched.

I was tempted to take advantage of Caroline's slightly elevated fear of sailing and say, "Yes! Keep your eyes open." But parental duty got the better of me. "Nah! This boat will have no problem at all."

"Whew!" she sighed. Soon Caroline joined the rest of the family in snoozeland.

Crosby's On the Starboard Side

Around 5:00 P.M. the sleepyheads began to stir and by 5:30, on approach to Osterville Harbor, everyone was awake, alert and ready for docking and dinnering.

The Crosby Yard lies just beyond the Osterville Bascule Bridge at the end of a double-bay journey through the West Bay Cut. Looking at the navigation charts, Ned remarked that this multiple-bay entrance looked all the world like a double-parlor lobster trap net arrangement. Be that as it may, the clearly marked channel helped considerably as we headed for the harbor's entrance. To either side of BUCKRAMMER, sandbars, mudflats and shoals poked up and about in random, unpredictable patterns. One wrong turn would put us "on the hard." These were waters made for shallow-draft catboats such as our old Crosby gem, or vice versa. We finally arrived at the bridge connecting the mainland of Osterville to the exclusive, gated community of Oyster Harbor on Little Island. The bridge was our last hurdle prior to entering "Crosby-town."

In advance of our trip, I had called the Crosby Yard, described our "Roots" expedition and reserved a slip. Jessica Steiner, one of the yard's managers, was delighted to hear of our visit. She promised to arrange a meeting and tour with the yard's current owner/managers, Dick Egan and his son Greg.

Once past the bridge, we approached the Crosby docks to starboard and hailed the wharfmaster on the radio. He directed us to a suitable overnight slip and within minutes, BUCKRAMMER settled in. After more than ninety years she had returned home once more.

Jessica, a trim, twenty-something, met us on the dock. She welcomed the family and explained the layout of the facilities (the historic worksheds had closed for the day), gave us directions into town and told us that the Egans would see everyone at 9:00 sharp the next morning. After a shower and a change of clothes, the Conway gang hit the road to walk the half mile or so into Osterville.

Founded in 1789, Osterville retains much of the charm of the "Olde Cape" (i.e., the Cape before the Kennedy era, when developers made Cape Cod a commuting suburb of Boston). Its shops, restaurants and museums offer an architectural integrity hard to find these days.

Jessica had told us of a pizza restaurant called Sweet Tomatoes and that's all the kids wanted (Chris and I were more inclined to sup at a little French spot called La Petite Maison but Abby, Ned and Caroline would have nothing of it.) On the way into town we had passed the Osterville Historical Society's museum grounds. After dinner, ice cream cones in hand, we walked back to the museum to see what hours it kept.

In my research on catboats I had constantly encountered references to the Osterville Historical Society. In 1975, the Society had physically moved the entire Herbert F. Crosby boatshop, tools and all, to the museum's grounds. Dating from the early 1900s, the boatshop was now the center of a three-building museum complex that chronicled both the history of the boatbuilding Crosby family and the catboats that they designed, modeled and built.

Abby raced to the front door of the main museum building and read the hours of operation from a card in the window. "10:00 A.M. to 4:30 P.M.," she yelled. I suggested that we could come back right after our visit with the Egans. The rest of the crew mutinied at this idea, however, and suggested that we could come back after a late morning and early afternoon sail and swim in Oyster Harbor. I agreed.

Back on the dock a few people had gathered next to BUCKRAMMER. As our family approached, one of them introduced himself and then asked if our boat was "the real deal." When I answered in the affirmative, the remainder introduced themselves and asked if they could examine the old floating woodpile.

"Of course!"

For the next hour or so, until darkness shut us down, a small stream of "lookers" came by to examine an authentic Crosby. We told and retold the ESTHER-JOSEPHINE S-PELICAN-CAPE GIRL-BUCKRAMMER history and allowed everyone to take a seat at the wheel, pull the lines, go below, try the bunks, poke the coal stove and twiddle the oil lamps.

As the last of the visitors departed, Ned offered, "Gee Dad, maybe we don't have to go to the museum tomorrow. We've got the 'real deal' right here." He was right! But I still wanted to check out the museum.

Captain Koop, I Presume?

We turned in around 10:00 P.M. and quickly drifted off; the salt air works wonders in the sleep department. Morning came sooner than we wanted and, feeling a bit lazy, we decided to head over to the Crosby Yard's restaurant, Keepers, for breakfast. Before long 9:00 A.M. rolled around, and we walked over to the office to keep our appointment with Dick and Greg Egan.

Jessica had told us to walk through the ship's supply store, past the old safe and up the stairs to the left. There we would find Dick's administrative assistant, Susan, who would announce us to the Egans' We followed Jessica's directions to the letter, pausing only to ogle the old, massive, floor-to-ceiling safe emblazoned with a boatbuilding mural and the Crosby name—what a piece of work! The well-worn staircase led to the owner's office one flight up. Banded with white-oak beadboard wainscoting, the stairwell was drenched with 100 years worth of spar varnish. Dozens of original, antique, half-hull models of catboats, power cruisers and racing craft, each about 18 to 24 inches in length, graced the walls. Every model had a four-digit number painted amidships; none was greater than 1935.

We reached the landing at the top of the stairs and introduced ourselves to Susan who sat behind a walled enclosure at a switchboard. She paged the Egans and invited us to make ourselves comfortable. The lobby in front of Susan's station, much like the stairwell, was lined with beadboard wainscoting and hung with even more half-hull models. An open door to our right revealed a large, skylighted room containing numerous drafting tables, drafting supplies, a large, wooden blueprint file case and dozens of additional half-hull models. The open door in front of us led to a paneled conference room, also skylighted, with numerous nautical artifacts such as a ship's wheel, an antique binnacle, more half-hulls and so on. A warren of rooms opened to our left, and a set of lavatories completed the layout. We scanned the offices over and over. It was as if the Conways had stepped into a time machine set for 1908. Even the light switches were odd-looking originals. Wow!

Susan broke the spell. "What do you think of our squeaky old place? It would be pretty hard to tiptoe quietly around here, eh?" She was right. The floors did add their own aural charm to the antique office.

"Hello I'm Dick Egan and you must be the Conways." A gentleman with grayish white hair and a C. Everett Koop–style beard exited the conference room and extended his hand. We introduced ourselves and Dick Egan continued.

"Let me show you around the offices here. Then I'll call

my son and he can take you down to the boatshops where your cat came to life."

The tour began in the drafting room. Dick told us that the boatyard had been sold to the first non-Crosby owner back in 1972. The Crosby family, he explained, wanted no part of fiberglass boatbuilding. The new owner discontinued any form of boat construction and focused on selling power cruisers manufactured by Uniflite Corporation. Unfortunately, that business lasted only four years before failing. This allowed Dick Egan to purchase the facility in 1976 "at a price more attractive than it would have been in 1972."

Egan immediately reenergized the boatbuilding business and began to produce a gaff-rigged fiberglass sloop called the Wianno Senior, a line of small harbor tugs, Striper fishing boats and yacht tenders. "I knew that I would not become a millionaire via boatbuilding," he said. "But it somehow

Crosby Marine President/CEO, Dick Egan, works surrounded by hundreds of half-hull models of small craft, mostly catboats, built over the 150 year's of the yard's existence.

seemed right to start building boats here again, at least on a break-even basis." He also set up a wooden and fiberglass boat repair business to "fill in the white spaces" between new boat construction jobs. More than twenty-five years later, the plan seems to have worked.

"My Dad ran a marina and it's really in my blood. We have good years and bad, but we make a reasonable living overall."

While still in the drafting room, Dick detailed what we saw. "You're surrounded by thousands of designs produced by generations of Crosbys over the years. The walls hold just a sample of the half-hull models used to design catboats, old power cruisers and other craft in the days before calculators and blueprints."

Egan explained that, prior to World War I, a typical Crosby design began as a 20-inch-long, 6-inch high stack of basswood slabs pinned together by wooden dowels. One of the Crosbys would whittle away at the stack with a sharp penknife and, literally, carve out the starboard-side profile of the proposed hull. During the whittling process, the carver would transfer years of past experience and extensive feedback from the owners of previous boats into each new design.

The finished model would be shown to the prospective owner for approval or adjustment. Once accepted, the model would then go down to the building crew. In the shop, the crew would carefully measure all of the critical dimensions of the model and, in a process known as lofting, scale the dimensions up to full size. To make it easier for the builders to derive measurements from the complex curves of the model, the model was taken apart into slices by simply removing the wooden pegs.

Abby asked, "Why did they only carve half of the boat and not the whole thing?"

"Yankee cheapness explains part of it," Egan replied. "But the main reason was that it would be very difficult for the carver to exactly duplicate both the right and left sides of the model. The boatbuilders only needed the dimensions of one side to build, so why waste the time?" Egan continued, "Have you noticed that each of the half-hull models on the walls contain a date?" We all nodded.

"That date is the year when that particular boat was built. The oldest here in this room is that racing catboat over there with '1898' painted on it." Opening a blueprint drawer, Egan pulled out a sheet of vellum showing fine pen-and-ink drawings of a small boat from numerous perspectives.

"When science began to take hold, even homebred designers such as the Crosbys abandoned the model-building approach and moved to the drafting table. This cabinet holds thousands of these drawings. Many of these were built, but many were not. Nowadays, all of this is done on a computer."

From the drafting room, Dick Egan led us into his conference room and personal office. Besides more half-hull models, the walls in these spaces held numerous photographs, taken from land, sea and air, of the Crosby Yard over the years. Egan pointed to a particularly large, aerial photograph of the facility.

"Before you go downstairs with Greg, I thought we'd take a look at this photo. Taken around 1938, it provides the best perspective on the layout of the shops. As you can see, the boatyard consists of a series of small, interconnected, wooden buildings. In the olden days, a Crosby brother, uncle or cousin each owned one of these and conducted his own business there."

Pointing to one of the structures in the photo, Dick continued, "Over the years and as appropriate, the Crosby relatives would bridge the spaces between the buildings with these enclosed connectors. With regard to your boat, we know for example that at some time in the early 1900s, Daniel and Charles teamed up and linked their respective shops together."

Egan took a pen from his pocket and pointed to one of the many buildings. "We refer to this boathouse as the North Shed. In all probability, this is where your boat was built back in ought-eight."

As we all gathered in for a closer look, it suddenly dawned on me that I was carrying the bound volume of *The Rudder*, which I had brought along as a reference. I opened to the page with the photos of the yard taken in "ought-six" and asked Dick if he had ever seen this article.

"I'm tempted to say that I've probably seen everything ever written about the Crosbys, but I can't recall ever having read something that far back in *The Rudder*." I put the book down on a nearby table and Dick examined the picture.

"Hmmm. Yes! See right here you have the North Shed, and there is Daniel's shop adjacent. Looks like they had not yet joined forces when this shot was taken."

"Hey everyone! Ready to see the shop? I've only got a little bit of time." Greg Egan popped out of his office and extended his hand.

We assured Greg of our "readiness" and gathered up behind him. Dick asked if Susan could make a photocopy of *The Rudder* piece while we were taking the shop tour. Saying that that was the least we could do, we thanked Mr. Egan, Sr. for his time and followed Greg down the stairs and into the shop bays.

For the second time in the same morning we enjoyed the eerie sensation of time travel, this time enhanced by the unmistakable fragrance of boatbuilding woods such as cedar, oak and yellow pine. Amazingly, the main shop looked like a photograph taken at the turn of the nineteenth century.

Running down the center of the shop was a marine railway that led to massive wooden doors and the waterfront beyond. Wooden workbenches and a wide variety of woodworking tools surrounded the railway on a wide-planked pine floor. To the right lay a large, ancient wood-burning stove. Overhead racks held boatbuilding wood, spars, sails and lines. The whole place was the stuff of a wooden boat builder's dreams.

"No sense dawdling in this new, Wilton Crosby, part of the operation," Greg said. "Dad says that Charles Crosby built your boat in the North Shed, a few buildings over to the right. Let's go!"

We looked at one another with raised eyebrows. The *new* part?

With Greg in the lead, we made our way through one of the connecting sections into what must have been Daniel's original shop. From within, the "connector" was a good-sized building in its own right, with numerous benches, tools and boatbuilding materials and supplies semi-neatly organized everywhere. Daniel's shop looked much like that of Wilton, only older. Here one tool in particular, a locomotive-scale band saw, caught my attention. Greg immediately noticed my reaction.

"Anyone who works wood has the same reaction when they stumble across that mechanical beauty. She'll handle any timber that we can throw at her like 'buttah.' I'd give you a demo but her blade is out at the sharpener." He continued, "So, you do work wood, eh?"

I explained that, as a willing-to-learn, rank amateur, yes, I had restored most of the BUCKRAMMER. This seemed to lighten up the junior Egan, who until then had exhibited a tad more intensity and impatience than his dad. Greg paused and smiled. "OK! Next stop Uncle Charlie's."

We Conway ducklings trailed behind Greg as he slid open a solid wooden door along its ceiling-mounted tracks and bounded into the old North Shed. After many years of owning BUCKRAMMER and promising myself that I'd come to Osterville some day, we would finally see the old girl's launching pad.

There's No Place like Home

For the next thirty minutes we roamed around the establishment of the man honored on the builder's plaque on our catboat: Chas. Crosby—Builder—Osterville.

Though set up much like the other shops that we had just passed through, with a railway in the center, flanked by benches and tools, and hard pine floors, Charlie's boatshop offered a more "high bay" design capable of accommodating vessels of greater depth and volume. The structure's post-and-beam architecture spoke volumes about the durability of this construction method.

I can't remember much of the conversation that transpired while we were in the shed. In fact, we probably did not say much. The place provided a sort of touchstone to the past, and all of us got lost in our respective reveries. I do remember taking many, many photographs, so many in fact that Ned warned me to save some film for the remainder of the trip.

While we explored the North Shed, Greg slipped into yet another connected building behind Charlie's and disappeared. After a while, he poked his head into "our" building and suggested that we might be interested in what the last building held. As a group we walked up the wooden ramp into what we would learn was the restoration shop. In a space a little smaller than the previous three shops on the tour sat two, antique, Wianno Senior racing sloops undergoing retrofits. One had her lowermost, or "garboard," planks removed to accommodate the replacement of some critical keel pieces with freshly machined teak or angelique. The other awaited a varnish and paint job.

Greg proudly puffed, "Tell your friends that the wooden boat business continues to this day at the old Crosby Yard. And that we hope to keep it this way for a good, long time."

On the reverse walk back to the senior Egan's office, Chris noticed that the now interior walls of the North Shed

within the connector still held their exterior white cedar or
green asphalt shingles. When asked, Greg matter-of-factly
replied that this was yet again an example of good, old Yankee thrift.

"I'm sure that the Crosbys thought, Why go through all
of the bother of stripping perfectly good siding away just to
connect a few buildings?"

Back in the office we retrieved our copy of *The Rudder*,
once again thanked Dick and Greg Egan, Susan and Jessica
and then headed back outside.

We all just milled around for a few seconds until Caroline piped up. "Well, that was something you don't see or do
everyday." We all broke into an emotion-relieving laugh and
quickly agreed with PD (our nickname for Caroline). This
had definitely been a unique morning.

Under our original plan, we would have spent the next
few hours "sailing and swimming" around Oyster Harbor.
But with the hour now close to noon and the history bug
still infecting the lot, we decided to walk back into town,
grab lunch at a hamburger place we had seen called
Wimpy's and then pay a visit to the Osterville Historical Society.

After a wonderfully greasy, fattening lunch, we strolled
back to the museum grounds. Museum Director Susan Mc-
Garry welcomed us as if we were part of her own family.
Sue convinced the ladies to tour those parts of the museum
grounds *not* devoted to boatbuilding, but rather to seven-
teenth- to nineteenth-century life in Osterville. Ned and I decided to pass on this and headed over to the boatshop area
of the museum. For the next hour everyone had a grand
time. The Osterville Historical Society is to be commended
for assembling and maintaining a remarkable collection.
Anyone interested in Cape Cod history can get much of the
story right here.

The Boat Shop Museum complex contains a number of
original Crosby catboats, several Wianno Seniors and Juniors

and a 1950s vintage Striper. The bulk of the collection focuses on the Crosbys through a well-organized series of historical photographs, countless original half-hull models and authentic displays of the boatbuilder's art. The museum filled in most of the voids in our understanding of the who's, what's, when's, where's, why's and how's of this remarkable clan.

Before leaving the boating museum buildings, Ned spied some initials discretely carved in the timber frames of the original Herbert Crosby portion of the building. This gave Ned a big, bad idea, which he shared with me.

"It would be risky, but worth a shot," I agreed. Execution of the plan would have to wait until our return to the boatyard.

Ned and I met up with the ladies, thanked Susan and her staff and then wandered back to the Crosby Yard.

Abby spoke up. "Hey Dad, it's only 3:00. Why don't we go for a sail and a swim like we had originally planned?"

BUCKRAMMER's birthplace, the Charles Crosby boat-shed in Osterville, Massachusetts (shown here in 2003), has changed little since the 1800's.

"OK!" I agreed. "But first Ned and I have a mission to accomplish." We explained the idea to the ladies. They thought we were wacky but would not do anything to stop us.

As Abby and Caroline prepared BUCKRAMMER for a quick getaway, I took out my pocketknife and sliced a small chunk out of BUCKRAMMER's keel from a spot beneath the floorboards near her centerboard trunk. Ned took this relic, jumped into SPLINTER and rowed over to the North Shed, where he dropped from sight. Ten anxious minutes later, Ned came back into view, climbed into our dinghy, rowed back to the mother ship and gave the thumbs-up signal. I helped him aboard and gave him a high five. The ladies just shook their heads and groaned, "What a bunch!"

"Did you have any problem?" I whispered.

"Yes. Let me explain. The side door was unlocked, just as we thought. I opened it a crack and seeing no one inside, went through. Just as I closed the door behind me, some very large guy came into the North Shed and I had to duck for cover behind one of the workbenches. The guy rooted around for a few minutes until he found whatever he was looking for and then left. I waited an extra few minutes, just to be sure that he would not return, then came out of hiding and did the dirty deed."

Within a small crack between the floorboards of Charles Crosby's North Shed lies a 2-inch sliver of BUCKRAMMER, one of the only surviving small craft designed, built and launched by that prolific practitioner of the vanishing art.

Appendix 1

——❧——

Restoration Program

Many readers of the BUCKRAMMER stories have written to ask how we manage to keep the old girl afloat. So I thought it might be useful to cover these topics in one place at one time.

Maintenance Program

We purchased the boat in 1993 and, as described earlier, had her surveyed by G. W. Full and Associates of Marblehead, Massachusetts, a firm considered among the very best at what they do. The surveyor, Paul Haley, prepared a detailed report that included a prioritized list of projects necessary to ensure that another eighty years or so would pass under her keel. We tackled these projects one by one, beginning with a reworking of the structural members of the boat's centerboard trunk and moving along from there. We vowed to have the boat safely in the water each year and, to date, have kept that promise.

In my experience, *old* wooden boats are certainly more maintenance-intensive than fiberglass craft, but not outrageously so. The key, as in all things mechanical, lies in one's ability to place the boat on a maintenance schedule and stick to it. If maintenance slides for a season or two with a wooden boat, the fix will require an exponentially more costly and time-consuming repair.

We have placed BUCKRAMMER on a recurring, ten-year program that covers all aspects of the boat, including hull planking and fastening, internal ribs and floors, cabin interiors and exteriors, spars, engine and accessory equipment. Anything that can be easily removed from the boat during the winter, such as the cabin doors, doghouse roof, skylight and so on, are removed, inspected and either touched up or rebuilt. It is far easier to make repairs and restore finishes in the comfort of the workshop over an entire winter; this approach turns what could be drudgery into something closer to washing the dishes or cleaning the house, i.e., no big deal.

The "Yard"

I have performed all of BUCKRAMMER's scheduled (and unscheduled) maintenance with one exception. This involved the replacement of the boat's main boom after her mainsheet fouled during a blow, resulting in the literal explosion of the original. This work, requiring special tools and exceptional craftsmanship, was performed by Warren Barker of Customary Boats in Westport, Massachusetts.

Do-it-yourself boat maintenance is not for everyone. In my case, a love of woodworking and woodworking machinery coupled with a modest boating budget (my kids' college education takes precedence) has me in the shop on a regular basis. However, my adventures and misadventures as an amateur boatwright offer almost as much fun as the boating itself (I said *almost*). Over the boating years, the Conways have also lived in no fewer than five homes, most built in the Victorian era or earlier. I have applied the skills gained in boat work to the maintenance and upgrade of these homes and have saved significant amounts of money on repairs as a result—or at least I keep telling my wife this.

Tools

Almost every book I have ever read on the subject of wood-working begins with an admonition along the lines that "you should buy the best tools available or none at all." My budget allows a "spend" of about $500 per year on wood-working tools and supplies. A reasonably stocked shop equipped with "all of the best tools" would cost around $10,000, about twenty years' worth of tool-purchasing on my budget. So what to do? Again, I let the long-term project list dictate things.

My first priorities were structural in nature and required the fabrication of fairly hefty timbers, ribs and keel pieces. One tool leapt to the front for this work, the band saw. So I broke down and purchased a Delta 12-inch saw for around $300. It became the core of my boatshop and I have never regretted the purchase. That first year I also purchased a Delta 10-inch benchtop saw for about $100 and a Porter-Cable orbital sander for about $100, also consistent with the long-range program.

Ten years and many excellent tools later—router, join-ter, planer, drill press, portable drill, dust collector and dozens of nonpowered hand tools such as chisels, planes and screwdrivers—I still covet a Delta cabinet saw but can-not justify the expense (about $1,500 new as of 2003). So I still use my original $100 bench-topper equipped with an exceptional Forrest 10-inch blade (highly recommended) and a homemade sliding table. The blade and the sliding table make up for the shortcomings of the bench saw in a BIG way.

Materials

Technology has smiled on wooden boat aficionados, such as myself, over the last ten years. The combination of new sealants, such as Sikaflex and 3M's 5200; new glue "systems" such as those offered by West System, System Three and others; and the ready availability of traditional boatbuilding woods such as white oak, cedar and yellow pine, as well as "new" woods such as angelique, ipe and okoume, has saved many old boats from the July Fourth town bonfire. Many of these products and materials are stock items at "big box" home centers such as Home Depot and Lowe's.

In addition, many of the materials used in the maintenance and restoration of my boat were salvaged from dumpsters outside of Victorian houses undergoing reconstruction projects in my local neighborhood and elsewhere. The white oak beadboard of BUCKRAMMER's galley formerly graced the walls of a kitchen in Winchester, Massachusetts. We lifted the yellow pine of our catboat's cockpit from the stairwell of a rehabbed home in nearby Lexington. The Douglas fir used in our skylight once served as the floor of a janitor's closet in an old schoolhouse in Boston. And so on.

Sources

Below is source information for many of the organizations, businesses and hardware items referred to in this book.

Information

Alibris (antique books)
www.alibris.com

Amazon (antique books)
www.amazon.com

Brattle Book Shop
9 West Street
Boston, MA 02111
Phone: 800-447-9595
www.brattlebookshop.com

Captain G. W. Full and Associates
46 Cedar Street
Marblehead, MA 01945
Phone: 781-631-4902
http://home.attbi.com/~captfull

The Catboat Association
www.catboats.org

Columbia Trading Company (used nautical books and antiques)
1 Barnstable Road
Hyannis, MA 02601
Phone: 508-778-2929
www.columbiatrading.com

Messing About In Boats (magazine)
29 Burley Street
Wenham, MA 01984-1943
Phone: 978-774-0906
www.messingaboutinboats.com

The Osterville Historical Society
www.osterville.org

WoodenBoat (magazine)
Box 78
Brooklin, ME 04616
Phone: 207-359-4651
www.woodenboat.com

Antique and Specialty Marine Hardware

Bristol Bronze
Box 101
Tiverton, RI 02878
Phone: 401-625-5224
www.bristolbronze.com

Jamestown Distributors
500 Wood Street, Building #15
Bristol, RI 02809
Phone: 800-423-0030
www.jamestowndistributors.com

J. M. Reineck and Son
9 Willow Street
Hull, MA 02045-1121
Phone: 781-925-3312
www.bronzeblocks.com

Lannan Gallery
540 Atlantic Avenue
Boston, MA 02110
Phone: 617-451-2650
www.lannangallery.com

Traditional Marine Outfitters
360 St. George Street, Box 268
Annapolis Royal, Nova Scotia
Canada B0S 1A0
Phone: 902-532-7634
www.traditional-marine.com

Boatbuilding Woods

Anderson and McQuaid
170 Fawcett Street
Cambridge, MA 02138
Phone: 617-876-3250
www.andersonmcquaid.com

Boulter Plywood
24 Broadway
Somerville, MA 02145
Phone: 617-666-1340
www.boulterplywood.com

Downes and Reader Hardwood Company
60 Evans Drive
Stoughton, MA 02072
Phone: 781-341-4092
www.downesandreader.com

Used Marine Engines, Parts and Advice

The Engine Room
Bryon Kass, President
Foxboro, MA
Phone: 508-543-9068

Appendix II

———✦✦✦———

Favorite Projects

BUCKRAMMER fans have also asked for details regarding a number of the improvements we've made over the years. As mentioned in Chapter 10, many of these projects were inspired by an exceptionally well-illustrated article found in the April 1906 issue of *The Rudder* magazine. The article describes the journey of the author, an editor at the *Rudder*, from Boston to the Crosby boatyards in Osterville. In the piece, the author inspects and photographs the exterior and interior of a Crosby catboat built on spec and available for sale (he buys it). It is likely that much of BUCKRAMMER's interior design, lost to a number of half-baked "restorations" over the years, is revealed in the tale. We have selectively used these layouts as guides for our own restorations.

Binnacle

The binnacle provides a central location for our ignition elements (starter and glow-plug switches), Danforth compass, Garmin GPS receiver, Lowrance depth-sounder system, and all engine gauges (Stewart Warner temperature, oil pressure

BUCKRAMMER's binnacle serves as the information center for the boat. The brass piping (at the base of the unit) provides structural support and also serves as the conduit for all wires and cables. This allows opening of the engine cover without interference.

and fuel level). It also provides a convenient place to hang a pair of binoculars and our spare, mouth-operated boat horn.

The unit is constructed as a hexagonal wooden (poplar) column capped with an antique hexagonal "light-house" binnacle fixture found in a now-defunct nautical supply shop within the South Street Seaport section of New York City. (Similar binnacle caps are now available from the Lannan Gallery in Boston.) All cables route through a series of brass tubes and knuckles mounted on the rear of the column. The brass tubes are lined with non-conductive corrugated plastic tubing, which provides a form of back-up insulation for the electrical wiring. This wires-through-the-tubing arrangement allows us to fasten the binnacle to the deck in such a way that it does not interfere with the removal of the engine covers.

Skylight

When we bought BUCKRAMMER, the front hatch consisted of little more than a canvas-covered, slatted wooden board. The board held a solar-powered ventilator that improved air circulation inside the cabin but did not admit any light. As a result, the interior cabin lived in a perpetual twilight state that encouraged mold and cold. Inspired by the "signature" skylight forward hatch of the Anderson Catboat Company, we decided to build one of our own. A skylight construction article in *WoodenBoat* magazine provided some guidance. At the time my lack of appropriate woodworking tools required improvisation. The base and window frame wood is old-growth Douglas fir salvaged from a building rehab. The window guard holders are white oak Beetle Cat rib stock. The bars are ¼-inch silicon-bronze bar stock, and the glass is ⅜-inch safety glass. The skylight connects to the boat by means of a very heavy-duty pair of bronze window risers and associated hardware salvaged by Traditional Marine Outfitters from a boneyard vessel in Nova Scotia.

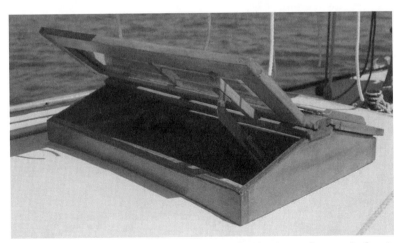

The skylight directs both light and fresh air (due to its fore and aft orientation) into the main cabin. It was easily built using simple tools.

The skylight windows open fore-and-aft rather than the more traditional port and starboard. This allows them to act as wind scoops while the boat is underway in sheltered waters or when she lies at anchor or on her mooring. Some have criticized the arrangement, but I actually checked with officials at the Mystic Seaport Museum prior to constructing the skylight in this configuration. They reported that several boats and ships in their collection had skylights oriented in this manner and therefore gave their blessing. Good enough for Mystic Seaport, good enough for BUCKRAMMER.

Galley Rehab

When we purchased the boat, her galley consisted of a number of waterlogged plywood and particleboard cabinets and countertops covered with Delft-reproduction ceramic tiles. In our third year of ownership, we decided to rip out all of this in order to restore the galley to a design more in keep-

The refurbished galley, constructed of salvaged white oak beadboard, provides an authentic, "ice-box" look and feel reminiscent of a design shown in a 1912 Rudder magazine article.

ing with the layout depicted in some photos taken inside of the Crosby catboat TWISTER in 1906.

In those "olden days" the galley area was quite open and sheathed with varnished, white oak beadboard for a look much like that of an antique icebox. To duplicate this effect, we first carefully measured the dimensions of the bulkhead walls and centerboard trunk sections that faced the galley area. These measurements were transferred to ⅜-inch, marine-grade okoume plywood. Cut into two, pattern-matching bulkheads, the plywood acted as a substrate for the beadboard.

In the comfort of my basement workshop during the winter, I milled the beadboard and glued and screwed it to the plywood. In the bulkhead section that would face the engine area, I made two cutouts and covered these with icebox-like doors, also made in my shop. Reproduction bronze icebox hardware completed the effect. Finally, I built and installed a varnished, bi-fold shelf that becomes our galley countertop when lowered but folds away for easy storage.

In the spring, I glued and screwed the prefabricated plywood-beadboard assemblies to the matching bulkhead or centerboard trunk wall areas. This approach resulted in easily constructed and maintained galley walls and storage that very closely duplicate the original crisp, clean, minimalist layout.

Fireplace

The original, Shipmate No. 2 coal stove sat high atop the galley counters when we took delivery of BUCKRAMMER in 1993. The 1906 photos show the stove much closer to the sole (this improves center of gravity) and surrounded by an insulating brick fireplace or firebox. To recreate this arrangement, I built an appropriately sized box from commercial, fire-resistant cement board. The lower edge of the box was scribed to conform to the turn of the bilge. The box was

The Shipmate #2 coal and wood burning stove sits atop a "brick-box." The box provides insulation from the hull and anchors the forward-end of the kitchen space.

bolted to the ribs that would lie beneath it with a series of stainless steel angle irons and stainless screws.

Next I clad the top of the box with fire-resistant antique bricks, pointed with fire-resistant grout. This formed an insulating platform upon which the stove would ultimately sit. The sidewalls of the box were clad with small pieces of oak beadboard to match the other walls of the restored galley area.

We reinstalled the stove on top of the finished firebox. Stainless turnbuckles, through-bolted into both the brick and cement board and backed with stainless backer plates, secure the thing to the firebox. Finally, the lowered position of the stove required the addition of a new section of rust-resistant flue pipe.

Biography

John Conway has sailed the waters of New England since 1960, when his parents gave him and his brothers an 8-foot pram with which "to explore." He has written about his boating adventures ever since. John's relationship with the 100-year-old Charles Crosby catboat BUCKRAMMER began ten years ago and continues today. Both the Conway family and the catboat operate from Westport Point, Massachusetts during the summer months. In the real world, John is an executive for an international sports marketing and management firm.